5⊙⊙

STO⊙⊙PLES
Office Tools for Hopeless Fools

Kevin Reifler, Nick Vacca,
and Adam Najberg

This catalog is the
property of
Ivana Bump
Asst. Operations Mgr:
DO NOT REMOVE
from my desk!!
Unless you want the cubicle
next to Harry in accounting
who eats his own nose hairs
and gives up bathing for Lent.
Thank you.

 ST. MARTIN'S GRIFFIN   NEW YORK

Disclaimer

This is a work of parody and satire.

It is fiction. Except for the satirical reference to, or parody of, public figures and entities, the names of individuals and companies appearing in this book are the products of the authors' imaginations or are used fictitiously and any resemblance to real people or companies is coincidental. Also, news items and other references to media coverage in this book are used fictitiously. The owners or holders of copyright, trademark, or other rights in the material used by the authors for purposes of satire or parody have not endorsed this book.

The people featured in the photographs in this book are models, and all of the photographs are used for illustrative purposes only.

Reference in this book to the Stooples.com Web site does not mean that St. Martin's Press sponsors or endorses anything that might be said there. St. Martin's Press has no control over, and is not responsible for, the content or policies of that Web site.

www.stmartins.com

LIBRARY OF CONGRESS CATALOGING-IN-PUBLICATION DATA

Reifler, Kevin.
    Stooples : office tools for hopeless fools / Kevin Reifler, Nick Vacca, Adam Najberg.
        p. cm.
    ISBN 0-312-34086-9
    EAN 978-0-312-34086-5
    1. Work—Humor. 2. Office equipment and supplies—Humor. I. Title.

PN6231.W644 R45 2005
818'.602—dc22
                                        2005047055

10 9 8 7 6 5 4 3

From "Under the Desk" of
Stooples CEO Donny Steintrumper

My Fellow Shareholders:

In the face of adversity, I like to recall the words of the great financier J. P. Morgan, who said, "If at first you don't succeed, try, try again. Hahahaha. You're all fired. Except you, Elizabeth. Say, that's a lovely corset you're wearing."

I'm pleased to tell you that Stooples has had an amazing year. Sales up! Profits up! Share price up! My bank account and *GQ* Most Eligible Bachelor rating up! If J.P. and Elizabeth were here, they would be green with envy. In fact, they'd be green with mold. Mary, get these dead people out of here.

Why was Stooples so successful? The answer is obvious. We weren't caught. Not once. Not by the S.E.C., the IRS, the CIA, Ashton Kutcher, the Jehovah's Witnesses, the guy who wanted to wash my windshield for a quarter, or the annoying lady in the elevator who asks everyone if they had a nice weekend. We were not caught on tape, on film, in the act, in the crosshairs, with our pants down, between a rock and a hard place, dirty-handed, napping, stealing from the cookie jar, moonlighting in a porn film (gay or otherwise), or having sex with a chicken.

So, rather than telling you how great my business plan is working, which would take like twenty pages, let's save a forest and run through a few highlights and key points over the last business year.

The strategy I implemented when I took over this company two years ago was to dump crappy inventory. Last year, as we expanded our business into seven countries, I expanded that, accordingly, to dump crappy inventory onto foreigners. It worked marvelously well. All of the gray plastic keyboard covers, the smiley-face Handi-Wipes for computer monitors, basic blue pens, and other schlocky stuff is now out of our warehouses, generating revenue and creating opportunities for new and exciting product lines.

New opportunities abound (note: thank Nana Ortega for the thesaurus). After discovering that my secretary wasn't around to serve me coffee one day because her mother died or something, I figured this must be a problem elsewhere, and got the boys in engineering working on a solution. The result: Our "Where Are My Lazy Employees?"campaign is already a winner among Fortune 500 executives.

A visit to the White House—besides bagging me a cool picture with the president—proved fruitful. Though I couldn't convince the leader of the free world to don a "Stooples Rocks" T-shirt for the photo, a little Photoshop magic and there he was, in a Stooples shirt. And we look like buddies, with his arm around my shoulders.

I wanted to mention to you that I picked up a few necessities this year, including a corporate jet and a semiprofessional basketball team.

Hey, people, I know what you and our miserly CFO de Krook are thinking. But you're wrong. My time is valuable, and after that one incident where I was accused of attempting to join the Mile High Club while we were still on the runway, I've been labeled an "international security risk" and "a man who makes high-pitched wheezy noises during sex." So you see, if you dollar-cost-average this out over the next fifteen or twenty or so years, I'm actually saving us money by not having to wait around at bars and airports trying to pick up women by offering them a year's supply of free paper clips.

And who could resist buying an up-and-coming team like the West Virginia Slags of the now-defunct Continental Basketball Association for $150,000? Sure, they don't have a league or anyone to play against, but that's just a temporary setback. What's exciting about this team is that management is in talks with Governor Byron "Inbred-Relative Tax" Stillwater to build a

Glaring Omission Sunglasses See page 24

Modeled by Stooples CEO Donny Steintrumper

new stadium in a bid to join the National Basketball Association. Planned is a goat-shaped Stooples Arena, with seating capacity of 52,000, 48 luxury boxes, and snack bars that offer local delicacies like chocolate-dipped roadkill and unpeeled boiled potatoes. In the meantime, we've scheduled some scrimmage games against vertically challenged teams for the coming year, including the Lewisburg Lilliputians, the Fayetteville Fetuses, and the Morgantown Miners Who Are Still in Coma.

We're being joined in our NBA bid by hip-hop artist P. Diddley, former WWF wrestler Diddley Squat, and Diddley Widdley supermarket baron Riddley Piddley III. We're confident their support and the demographics will work in our favor. West Virginia's local television market is 279th in size, as long as you count the squirrels. The area is unfettered by competition from any other forms of professional entertainment, except for the Deliverance Reenactment festivals that typically attract few tourists. The Slags would draw its fan base from the Greater Kentucky-Virginia-Ohio triangle, the Tennessee-Ontario-Albania rectangle and a parallelogram in southern Mississippi. We also expect significant support from the squirrels.

And what great office-supply company is without a great corporate yacht? Yes, that's right. I bought a 125-foot yacht I renamed *Trump This* for $1.7 million at a government auction of seized assets from a Colombian low-carbohydrate drug dealer. I have her berthed down at the Potonquet Marina in Atlantic City, New Jersey, so if you're ever in the area, check out the Olsen Siamese Twins show at the Tropicana. Or put all your mortgage money on red 17. Just stay away from my boat.

We carried out several promotions this year. Proving that purchasing managers aren't CEOs for good reason, we successfully implemented our "Buy One, Get the Second at Full Price" program. We also found our practice of offering corporate executives a night with a "best practices, sex consultant" at New York's Plaza Hotel did wonders in our hunt for business from blue-chip companies. Thank you IBM, GE, Time Warner, Dow Chemical, and all the other big companies whose CEOs cared enough to buy the very best. And a word from Cherry "VaVoom"

Vaneshka to Microsoft's You-Know-Who: "Don't worry, sweetie. It happens to every high-tech billionaire from time to time."

Looking ahead to the current year, what can you expect? I'm excited to tell you that we're starting production in China, Malaysia, and Indonesia, having found reasonably priced child labor. We also plan to outsource production to other planets as soon as we can find aliens who will work cheaper than the Chinese and won't try to eat our executives or turn them into zombies or burst through their chest cavities with baby aliens.

And remember, Stooples is the proud winner of the Leonard R. Schumacher Award three years running. In the coming months, we plan to find out just who Leonard R. Schumacher really is and why he keeps leaving aluminum statues in our lobby. But we are sure they are well-deserved, and Stooples remains poised to kick the stuffing out of evil competitors OfficeHacks and OfficeDespot. We've got cash, we've got good products, we've got a strategy, a sports team, a ship, and, most important, we've got me, your CEO. I'm hellishly cute, multitalented, and I don't make high-pitched wheezy noises during sex. I won't let you down. I sell, therefore I am!

Onward and upward,

Donny Steintrumper

Donny Steintrumper

Fanny Pants

NEW!!

It's a long way from the top. Padded posterior on long-wearing worsted-wool trousers provide soft, happy landings. Slacks have multi-layered knee patches in case you go headfirst. Backside is doubly secured—inflatable air bag has room for immediate cash settlements! SKU **BUTT**

Save $5

$19.99 EACH
Reg. $24.99

Save $10

$39.99
Reg. $49.99

WoidPerfect

Want to write and sound like an Italian mobster? Looking for that certain South Brooklyn chic? WoidPerfect creates correspondence meant to intimidate, cajole and otherwise portray you as an unhinged, murderous lowlife, or at least a state senator from New Jersey. Automatic translation capability turns the Queen's English into gibberish as easy as one-two-tree. SKU **PESCI**

Save $5

$3.99
Reg. $8.99

Water Fountain Nasal Deflector

Don't let high-pressure fountains shoot water up your nostrils. Form-fitting guard lets you drink without worry or ducking. Plastic casing won't rust with repeated dousings. Comes in a variety of flesh colors for inconspicuous wear around the office. Specify Petite, All-American or Deluxe Honker. SKU **SPRITZ**

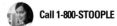
5

Kill Bill Collector Part II

Don't slam
bill collecto
tracks. Kill E
the harassm
gets started
plastic hand
ceramic tube
50,000 volts
directed burs
improves upo
no scorching
organs. Teste
paramedics a
your bill colle
from a myoca
DEBTFREE

Take two and double your lawsuit!

$29⁹⁹

Euro-Nal

Now French, Spanish and English people can all pee in the same place. No more complex Belgium urinals confusing Portuguese citizens who give up and take a leak on the floor. Now available: Extra-wide model perfect for indecisive EU members and the easy-to-fluster East Bloc. SKU **OUI PEE**

ONLY
$299⁹⁹

NEW!

Peel off label when ready to use

Empty Carton In the Hall Litigation Kit

Empty Carton in the Hall Litigation Kit

That carton has been sitting there for days, and you almost tripped over it twice. A nuisance? Or perhaps your opportunity for big bucks! Our turnkey, do-it-yourself litigation kit will help you stage a slip-and-fall that can provide millions to you, your lawyers, their wives, their ex-wives, their future mistresses, their various partners in money-losing ventures, their advertising agencies and many others whom we'd rather not mention. Kit comes complete with fake blood, real blood, hatchet-in-head Halloween mask, fake eyeball with extra rolling action, witnesses, expert witnesses, witless witnesses and many other things that we'd rather not list. Million-dollar settlement or your money back. SKU **NOTSAY**

$1,000⁰⁰
per carton

Visit us online @ **www.stooples.com**

 Call 1-800-STOOPLE

Extra Vowel Key Board

There's nothing worse than when you "oooh" and "aaaah" and then run out of vowels in midmemo. Our ergooonomically designed keyboard places extra As, Es, Is, Os, and Us strategically around the keyboard. Eliminates stupid keys like { and fractions. And what's with that ^ key anyway?

SKU **SOMETIMES Y**

$**64**⁴⁹

Gratuitious Floor Signs

Rectangular-frame floor sign lets you say it politely: "Smoking in Designated Areas Only," "This Is Not a Designated Area," "Nope Not Here Either," "Please Watch Your Step, Asshole," "Caution Wet Floor—Oops," "Please Seat Yourself," "Please Immolate Yourself," "Authorized Personnel Only," "Who Said You Were Authorized?" "Unauthorized Drugs Prohibited," "Authorized Drugs OK." Ornate lettering blends nicely with classier surroundings. Weighted base handy for those who don't listen. SKU **THANX**

$**12**⁹⁹

Please Watch Your Step, Asshole

Elbow Extender

Crowded? Elbow Extenders let you bulldoze your way through commuter throngs so you can catch your train. Creates "personal space" on elevated platforms or on densely traveled sidewalks. Helps you escape street violence and cocktail chatter. Available in Jim Brown, Mean Joe Green, Black and Blue All Over.

SKU **TRAMPL**

NEW
Low Price
$**33**⁰⁰

Executive Heart Attack Simulation Kit

Save $20

$299⁹⁹
Reg. $319.99

What's wrong with eight months' disability leave, anyway? Executive Heart Attack Simulation Kit includes EKG, bottle of Hollywood Sweat, red-face applicator and pocket-size noise box for real squealing and grunting ambience. Also available: Stroke Simulator, Ebola Outbreak, Irritable Bowel Believer. SKU **OUTTAHERE**

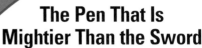

The Pen That Is Mightier Than the Sword

Now you can test this adage for yourself. Charge into battle wailing and flailing your pen against master swordsmen, knife-wielding psychos, manicurists with attitude and others armed with sharp weaponry. Not enough of a challenge? Take on Bloods and Crips, Peruvian rebel bases and Libya. Still not enough of a challenge? How 'bout I beat you upside the head with this book! SKU **IDIOT**

WILLIAM HANOVER 1897-1989

NEW Low Price

$299⁹⁹

All Time Low

49¢ EACH

Test the old adage out yourself!

Founder Bust Accessories

Company founder look like an old fud? Stylish designer hair and accessories keep his lobby bust from becoming a sartorial embarrassment. Impress clients with his "with-it" vitality—even if he's been dead for a hundred years! Handsome accessories resistant to both fire and tweaking by disgruntled employees. SKU **HIP**

8   **STOOPLES** Office Tools for Hopeless Fools   Visit us online @ **www.stooples.com**   Call 1-800-STOOPLE

Anal-Retentive Pocket Planner

Real executives don't stop with just a day planner. Our cushy-padded, leather-smelling, in-your-pocket planner lets you map your day five minutes at a time for maximum attentiveness. Note each thrilling meeting retort, bathroom break, wrong number and the time the small paper clips fell into the large paper-clip compartment and you had to spend ten minutes rearranging them. Special notes column lets you record daily attire, lunch choices, specific peppy greetings to the boss and who you cc'd versus who you bcc'd. A fine accompaniment to any neurosis. SKU **PICKY**

ONLY $24⁹⁹

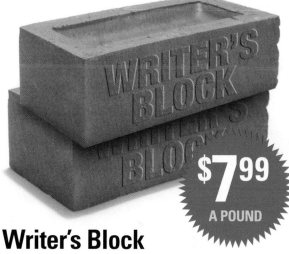

$7⁹⁹ A POUND

Writer's Block

Large block of granite is perfect for smashing writers who can't even perform the simple task of placing vowels and consonants together. Just imagine if these people had to get a real job, for Chrissakes! "Oh, no, I have to write, I wish I had an easy job like dismantling ticking explosives or performing gynecological services at the Fulton Fish Market." In fact, take half off and beat them twice.

SKU **SHAKESPEARE**

Salary Mugs $9⁹⁹ EACH

Why stop with initials and titles? Handsome coffee mug tells everyone what they pay you. Mug construction reflects your success: Basic Ceramic—to 75K, South American Onyx—to 150K, and Renaissance Marble for the above and beyond. Cheery hourly wage cups, in sturdy Styrofoam, available for those on the bottom rung. Optional four-prong desk stand holds mug high over desk for quick visitor perusal. SKU **MUG**

NEW!!

Portable Urinal Privacy Slats

Don't be intimidated by nosy onlookers. Portable wooden slats attach to any ceramic wall, obstruct view from the side, let you concentrate on the business at hand without embarrassment. Hemp rope handle allows unobtrusive carrying to and from office. SKU **PPSLAT**

$39⁹⁹

Security Badge Photo Distracter

Hate your security badge ID photo as much as the one on your driver's license ("Hello, a ferret is eating my small intestines.")? Our Security Badge Photo Distracter will take the focus off your demented expression and on to the action surrounding your photo. Choose from dogs chasing cats, kids chasing cats, Mr. Katz chasing Mrs. Katz, nuclear explosion over Nagasaki, Japanese chasing cats (postnuclear meal preparation), and ferrets chasing small intestines. Not recommended for pretty boys who live off their looks or those on the other end of the spectrum where it really doesn't matter anyway. SKU **KATZ MEOW**

$4⁹⁹ EACH

Schizophrenic Name Tags

Even schizophrenics need an introduction. Pressure-sensitive badges note psychological affliction: "Hello, our names are…" Keeps everyone from slighting either party. Bold blue vertical line separates names, guards against jealousy and bruised feelings. Also available: Paranoid Name Tags – both sides adhere for quick immersion of identity. SKU **US**

$2⁰⁰ Pack of 50

STOOPLES
Office Tools for Hopeless Fools

 Visit us online @ **www.stooples.com**

 Call **1-800-STOOPLE**

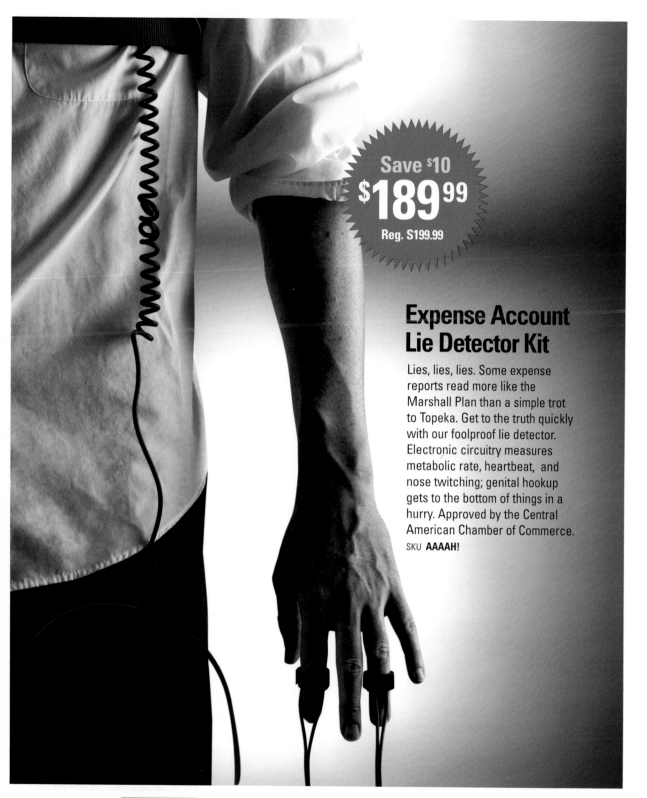

Save $10
$189.99
Reg. S199.99

Expense Account Lie Detector Kit

Lies, lies, lies. Some expense reports read more like the Marshall Plan than a simple trot to Topeka. Get to the truth quickly with our foolproof lie detector. Electronic circuitry measures metabolic rate, heartbeat, and nose twitching; genital hookup gets to the bottom of things in a hurry. Approved by the Central American Chamber of Commerce.
SKU **AAAAH!**

Albatross Beeper

Colorful electronic albatross beeper is a handy yet symbolic communications link to the office. The beeper box is surgically implanted in the bird's craw, creating realistic beak movements when set off. Digital readout in plumage gives you the correct number to call. Appropriate for executives and Ancient Mariners on the go. Also available: Pinpointing Pigeon, Grating Grebe, Cuckoo for Coco Puffs. SKU **BEEP**

NEW
Low Price
$59⁹⁹

Save $10
Reg. $69.99

Save $20
$59⁹⁹
Reg. $79.99

Salesman GPS Underwear

You may say you're with clients in Cleveland, but you could be anywhere. How does management know you're not dozing in Dallas, dillydallying in Detroit or getting a sex change operation in San Francisco (well maybe that one they'd know). Now management never has to wonder, thanks to Global Positioning System (GPS) Underpants. Reliable satellite tracking device fits neatly on elastic band, emits warning signal if removed before 7:00 p.m. Need to shower midday? Too bad! Cotton undies dry in minutes, leaving you slightly chapped but at management's beck and call. Available in Boxer, Brief, Panty or SexChangeSensitive Thong. SKU **YOU THERE**

5¢
FOR JUST ABOUT ANYTHING

OutSauce

Why use expensive American sauce on your business lunch when you can get it from other countries at a fraction of the cost? OutSauce is made by culinary professionals in India, China and other countries willing to make sauce for 97% less than what we charge here.
So what if our people lose their jobs and cost the government billions in unemployment and welfare payments. You get cheap sauce, and isn't that what life is all about? **Coming Soon:** OutSoup, OutS'mores and tantalizing OutHead. SKU **SHORTSIGHTEDBASTARD**

Key Moments in Stooples History

It's almost a cliché to say a company has "come a long way," but Stooples—the world's fastest-growing office-supply company—actually has. Our roots lie in Pakistan, the disputed Jammu-Kashmir region bordering India, to be precise. That's where our founder, border guard Mohammad Uq, took a bullet in his left butt-cheek in 1989 and accepted early retirement. That's where our history began.

Returning to the family hovel in downtown Karachi, Uq got an urgent phone call from his brother-in-law, Fuqed. "Brother," his brother-in-law chirped. "You must come quickly. I need your help. And bring your gun." Fuqed, a well-known fence in northern New Jersey, had received a load of hijacked office supplies and was racing ahead of the police and the Italian mafia to unload the products before he could be arrested or castrated. He had arranged a meeting to sell the supplies but wanted his brother-in-law there to provide protection. Kissing his wife and children good-bye, Mohammad hopped on a plane and was in America in twenty-four hours.

Amazing Miracle Listening Glass
See page 17

Well, the buyer never showed, but that didn't faze Mohammad. Scraping together his life savings and selling his second daughter to a prominent Pakistani businessman, Mohammad Uq bought those pens, pads, paper clips, and staplers from his brother-in-law; set up a storefront in downtown Newark's beautiful O'Leahy Building; and went into business. It took some time to get things right. He first named the business "Uq O'Leahy's," but after the fourteenth Hawaiian tourist in a month came in looking for Don Ho, he changed the name.

While Uq didn't really have a good grasp of marketing or English spelling—he renamed his company "Offus Stuf"—he did have a flair for the office-supply business. He sold off that first illicit load in seventy-two hours by selling at cut rates to local businesses. With his proceeds, he bought his first load of legal office supplies and was on his way. Within two years, he had expanded to a three-story building in Passaic, bought two warehouses, and was employing twenty-two family members, generating $230,000 in annual sales. Business leveled off at that point, and Mohammad Uq ran himself a pretty nice, albeit unspectacular, office-supply company over the next decade.

Life is full of coincidences. Just a few blocks away from Mohammad Uq's first store lived fifteen-year-old Donny Steintrumper, the man behind Stooples's meteoric rise to the middle of the global office-supply market.

He was born Julio Mayaguez Flamingo, son of poor immigrants from El Salvador. His mother was a sailor, ashore on a three-day pass. Julio spoke with a heavy accent mocked by classmates, especially because his accent was Swedish. His father worked eighteen-hour shifts cleaning houses. "I clean toilets so you don't have to," his dad told him. "Now, I'm going to work. Make sure you clean the toilet." Julio grew up in a time of rapid economic expansion in America and realized early on that money and status were the keys to everything. First, he ripped off the names of his heroes, a boisterous baseball-team owner and a rich man with a bad hairpiece. Then he decided the fastest way to riches of his own was to sell stuff.

Earthworms for bait, cold beer to construction workers, telephone cable he "found" while the repairmen were on a lunch break, doughnuts to the cops who arrested him for that misdemeanor, from the time he could count Donny sold anything that wasn't bolted down. He demonstrated an uncanny instinct for what people wanted at any given time, always selling the right product to the right people and always getting the price he wanted.

"I sell, therefore I am," Donny once said, a credo he has since lived by.

In high school, he was voted "most likely to sell the furniture in the teachers' lounge," something he actually did while in the tenth grade. Alas, Mr. Guilford, the gym teacher, saw him spiriting a chair out of the room and turned him in. Donny was suspended for weeks, which taught him something he has remembered to this day: Make others an accessory to your crime.

Testimony Helper

Helps you obscure even the most basic details during cross-examination

120 Minutes
2 DVDs

Testimony Helper See page 88

Today, all employees at any Donny Steintrumper–owned business own a tiny amount of company stock, whether they want to or not.

Donny carried his near-religious hustle into college. He worked days and attended Pace University at night, graduating with a bachelor's degree in business administration. Former classmates still remember him fondly.

"Sure. I remember him," said Hugo Jones, who took a requisite American history course with Steintrumper in their freshman year. "I bought a final paper from him. I got a C-. It was pretty expensive, and he didn't have his facts straight. I should have known George Washington didn't cross the Delaware on the *Niña, Pinta*, and *Santa Maria*. And the slave traders paid with rum, not American Express. I think I'll go to Stooples and ask for a refund."

During the day, Donny practiced what he studied, selling first brushes, then shoes, then shoe brushes, until he finally stumbled, with Steintrumper-like luck—or was it foresight?—into the area that would eventually make him a billionaire: technology. In 1995, personal computers were taking off, and the nineteen-year-old Donny found himself a job selling custom-made units to bored and lonely housewives who needed daily "service calls." Exhausted—and tired of being called "stud muffin"—Donny saved his money. Within two years, he launched a successful hostile takeover of the business. Suddenly, Donny Steintrumper was a CEO.

Steintrumper's first company, Fell-Off-the-Back-of-the-Truck Computers, was a $1.7-million-a-year business by the time he graduated from Pace in 1998. Shortly before donning his mortarboard, Donny the millionaire made his first-ever, but certainly not his last or most generous, philanthropic gesture, funding the $10,000 annual "Donny Steintrumper Get Up and Go" scholarship, awarded to the Pace University student who displays the most values of his or her benefactor. Coincidentally, Steintrumper was named valedictorian of his graduating class, cited by fellow students and professors for his "incredible charm, charisma, and boyish good looks."

"I think every graduating class in every generation should have a Steintrumper, be he—or she—black, white, slanty-eyed, a greaser, hebe, or whatever," Donny said during his valedictory address.

After college, Steintrumper had another insight.

"Get 'em to buy repeatedly and often," he told *Business Week*. "And the best and cheapest place to get the buying going is on the Internet. Bricks and mortar are dead, man."

Nature's Stress Balls See page 29

In June 1998, he moved into database software and the Internet. Working with a programmer, he developed proprietary database applications that matched single men and women on the basis of their food preferences. That turned into a national chain of computer-dating franchises called YouAreWhatYouEat.com, a business that was netting $50 million a year by the end of 1999.

"It was a great business," Donny told the *New York Times* in a March 1999 interview. "People who both love Chinese food typically share many other passions, such as fortune cookies and those little moist towelettes. And the best thing is, an hour later they're coming back to us."

Capitalizing on his company's rising profile, Donny soon spun off other successful dating services, including YouLikeTheMetsMeToo.com, HeyLetsComparePiercings.com, and IdenticalBurningSensations.net.

Donny's dating empire went public in January 2000. By the time global stock markets imploded in March 2000, Donny was already a billionaire and long gone from the company, having sold it to AOL for $1.6 billion, along with the Brooklyn Bridge for $1.2 billion, and the secret of invisibility for $1.1 billion.

"Man do I miss those AOL guys and their money," Donny told *Forbes* magazine in a recent interview. "Erectile dysfunction or not, that Dick Parsons sure knew how to spend his shareholders' money."

Back in his old Newark neighborhood in early 2001, Donny was feeling bored when he walked past Mohammad Uq's original Offus Stuf storefront and peered inside the dusty window. And in an instant, Stooples was born.

"I almost popped a woody," Donny told the Stooples employee newsletter. "I looked in there, saw these stacks of notebooks and boxes of those plastic folders and other office crap, and it was like destiny or an epiphany or *Carmen* or something. This wacky Paki was sitting on a gold mine and didn't even know it. I mean, jeez, everybody uses pens."

Offus Stuf found itself close to insolvency when tech markets collapsed. Uq had also correctly forecast that the technology market would take off in the 1990s and moved his company into furniture and fittings, in addition to office supplies. Only trouble was that by March 2000, nearly 95 percent of his contracts came from technology companies. Most were soon unable to pay their bills. Inventory piled up. So did invoices from wholesalers. Mohammad Uq was too leveraged. On June 1, 2001, he sold his company for $230,000 to Donny Steintrumper.

Steintrumper's first order of business was to rename the company.

Kama Sutra PDA See page 45

"We needed something that screamed, 'That's right! We do office supplies!' Or at least, 'We're Americans, and we can actually spell!' All the good names were taken, so we just kind of made some stuff up that sounded vaguely officey," he told the company newsletter. "Stooples it was. Ain't it original?"

He sifted through sales figures and inventory and made a snap decision to lay off all of Uq's family members, bringing in salespeople who worked purely on commission to off-load the old products piled up in Uq's warehouses. He kept Uq himself on as a security guard, because Uq had a gun.

Direct sales were passé, though, Donny knew. And, by that time, the Internet had made more people sick than his mother's cooking, so that was out as a primary sales point. The key, he realized, was a catalog.

"Every worker works in an office," Donny told the newsletter. "And every office has an office-supply catalog floating around. Everyone waits for them to show up, wants to read them, loves to tell the office manager, 'Yo, homes, we need more pens, more Post-its, yada yada."

Donny went out and bought a small printing house and devoted its entire production capacity to turning out Stooples catalogs—100,000 of them per printing—so that he could flood America's offices from coast to coast.

Time Sheet Pillow Cases See page 117

By August, Stooples was already back in the black. Creditors got their money; inventories were reduced. Stooples added staff by the dozens. That's when Donny decided to have some fun. And we're glad he did, because he forever changed the face of office supplies.

"Office supplies are boring, but it doesn't have to be that way. We spend so much of our time in those cubicles, drinking flat water from the cooler, putting toilet paper on the seat 'cause some guy before us peed on it. 'Damn,' I told my staff. 'Let's make office supplies exciting, something you again want to steal from your company and bring home to your kids.'"

Fun office supplies were a big hit.

Stooples went public at $1.90 a share on January 3, 2002. Because it wasn't a technology company, because it sold products every office needed, it was one of the few bright spots on Wall Street during the year. Its share price tripled by year-end and tripled again by the end of 2003.

We at Stooples would like to tell you that this story has a happy ending. But we can't because we're still growing and going strong, our annual sales rising at a triple-digit clip, our product lines expanding, and our reach into global markets extending into several new countries each year.

And our founder, Donny Steintrumper, is still at our helm. Yes, he sometimes hits inappropriately on female staff, yes, he stuffs Kleenex into his jockey shorts. Sure, he makes impulse buys of expensive things like basketball teams and boats and corporate jets, but he's the only man for this job.

No matter the intense competition of evil competitors OfficeHacks and OfficeDespot, we continue to depend on our young and charismatic leader to lead us to ever-higher levels of growth, service, and profitability. Either that, or it's back to cleaning toilets.

Deadwood File

The high cost of office space leaves little room for sentiment. Luxurious pullout drawers are just the answer for executives past their prime. Roomy interior allows placement of ledgers and telephone, contains shelving for mementos of successful days gone by. E-Z Roll ® wheels allow closet-to-closet maneuverability on a daily basis. SKU **PASTURE**

Save $10

$69⁹⁹

Reg. $79.99

Amazing Miracle Listening Glass

Want to hear everything being said in the next cubicle? Amazing Miracle Listening Glass lets you know immediately what your neighbor yells into the phone. Place Listening Glass against cubicle wall…you'll be amazed at the clarity of screams, loud threats and curses aimed at ex-boyfriends and the IT department. Comes in three comfortable sizes: Petite, Normal and Dumbo. Optional Electronic Monitor helps you detect sweet nothings, phone sex and heavy breathing. SKU **YENTA**

Save $3

$4⁹⁹

Reg. $7.99

Orgy in the Conference Room Spray

Save $10

9⁹⁹

Reg. $49.99

partners
passion
ates hot
date, jelly
aranteed
at least a
Odorless
urns wet
you will

Someone must be sleeping with our buyer!

I.B.

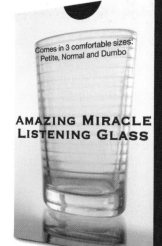

Comes in 3 comfortable sizes: Petite, Normal and Dumbo

AMAZING MIRACLE LISTENING GLASS

Want to **hear** everything being said in the next cubicle?

Optional Electronic Monitor helps you detect sweet nothings, phone sex and heavy breathing.

Punish those cities that won't buy your product!

$9⁹⁹
PER REGION

Marketing Voodoo Maps

Punish those cities and towns that won't buy your products. Haitian map and stick pins let you avenge the destruction of your marketing plans from the comfort of your own office. Create pestilence in Peoria, famine in Fargo, terror in Tenafly or just plain havoc in Honolulu. Comes with FDA-approved antidote for accidental finger pricks. SKU **WHODOO?**

ONLY $8⁹⁹

Coffee Ring Stamper

It may be 150 pages long, but your boss expects you to finish reading that report by morning. Self-inking coffee ring stamper shows you've put in your time—even if you haven't gotten past page three. Control settings create ten different rings for added credibility. Specify caf, decaf, latte or double decaf latte caf. SKU **SKIM**

18

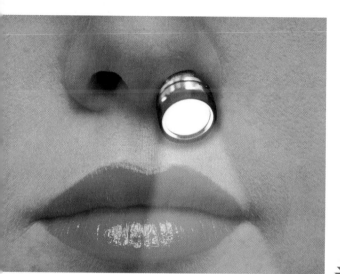

GREAT MOMENTS
IN OFFICE HISTORY

234 B.C. Paper clip invented by courtier of Emperor Ping of China's Ming Dynasty.

233 B.C. Paper invented to put in paper clip. Emperor Ping apologizes for putting courtier to death for stupid invention.

127 B.C. First instant text message written in sand by Roman with big stick.

126 B.C. First Roman sexual harassment suit filed; instant text messages subpoenaed.

125 B.C. Sand text messages uncovered by sand forensics experts, used as evidence against Emperor Nero. Emperor really burned up about it.

10 B.C. First office Christmas party. No one attends. Host stymied as to reason.

A.D. 2 First successful office Christmas party.

1062 Nostrodamus foresees great wars, nuclear weapons, and decorative boxes dispensing orange facial tissues at the bottom so you won't run out.

1564 Marquis de Sade invents office chair.

1673 Slave traders invade West Africa, trading gold and rum for cleaning people.

1773 Benjamin Franklin says pen is mightier than the sword.

1776 Private Leverhorn of the Colonial army dies attempting to attack British regiment with quill pen and pewter inkwell.

1898 Factory worker Rusty Tillerman punches office clock on way in, stopping time and breaking his fifth metatarsal. Observant office inventor develops working model of first punch clock, but is later executed by CEO Ping.

1912 First Karpel tunnel reported, as ten-year-old Jan Karpel digs twelve-foot crevice under home to escape washing goats.

1945 Tojo, Hitler skip annual office Christmas parties.

1998 U.S. President Bill Clinton requests extra padding for office chair for unknown reasons, renames Oval Office "The Marquis's Playpen."

2073 Robotic CEO Ping changes "Profit by Execution" policy to "Profit OR Execution." Productivity increases 700 percent!

Sissy Wrist Rests

Let everyone know what a wuss you are as you lay your dainty wrists on our durable, Lycra™-covered sissy rest. And what about your butt? You'd better rest that, too, with our smooth, inflatable, polymer butt rest. And what about your head when you take a nappy? Our gelatin-covered desk will keep you from hurting your head if you lay it down too quickly. OK, are we covered? Thank you. SKU **WIMP**

Save $3

$9⁹⁹
PAIR
Reg. $12.99

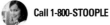
21

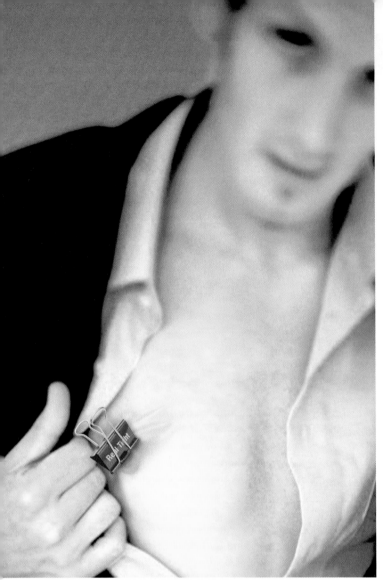

Sales Staph

Stop pesky sales reps in their tracks. Viral infection attacks larynx, neutralizes sales patter before it strikes. Cost-efficient bacteria work wonders with purveyors of insurance, office machinery and Girl Scout cookies. Portable dispenser great for the mall, airport Krishna-baiting, etc. Aerosol or liquid. SKU **PSST**

Only
$11⁹⁹

See the results in
just 48 hours

NEW
Low Price
$39⁹⁹

Versatile Office Nipple Clips

Many steel-tempered, nickel-plated binder clips are good for either gripping reports or clamping nipples, but never both. Until now. Our rectangular design holds paper, nipples, with equal efficiency and optimum compression. Durable grasp doesn't weaken over time or tugging. Option: you may remove arms for permanent binding, but think carefully. SKU **REAL TIGHT**

ONLY
39¢
EACH

Entremanure

High-energy nutrient encourages instant corporate revitalization. Powerful odor encourages staffers to look for ways to rapidly improve the working environment. Liberally sprinkle five-pound bag and watch the entrepreneurial spirit take root! Especially appropriate for companies where it's about to hit the fan anyway. Another fine product from Corporate Culture Laboratories. SKU **PHEW!**

 STOOPLES
Office Tools for Hopeless Fools

 Visit us online @ **www.stooples.com**

 Call **1-800-STOOPLE**

$salary and % of winnings negotiable

Vegas CFO

Any financial officer can deliver timely financial statements, cash forecasts and budget reports. It takes Vegas CFO to make your money work all night long at crap tables, roulette wheels and slot machines up and down the strip. Why settle for balance sheet valuations when you can double down at Blackjack Table Number Three? Vegas CFO knows when to hold your money, and when to fold before the auditors arrive. Double your company's cash reserves overnight, as long as you're feeling lucky.

SKU **HITME**

Gift Certificates

Give your friends, coworkers and family Stooples Gift Certificates all year round!

$10.00 Gift Certificate $20.00
$50.00 Gift Certificate $20.00
$100.00 Gift Certificate $2,000,000.00

(Sorry, we are temporarily out of $50.00 Gift Certificates)

STOOPLES
Office Tools for Hopeless Fools

Glaring Omission Sunglasses

Sometimes you forget. But does Wall Street care you had gum surgery the morning you forgot to announce earnings were off 43 cents a share? No, Wall Street does not give a poop. Protect yourself from the harsh light of glaring omissions with our 100% UV "refraction action" Glaring Omission Sunglasses. Makes fashion statements rather than mea culpas. Polarized lenses reflect tough questions. Flexible, amorphous frame easily withstands rigors of stock price collapse. A must for the cutting-edge executive in freefall. SKU **S.E. SEE**

NEW
Low Price
$6⁹⁹
Reg. $10.99

$39⁹⁹

Annual Report Crossword Puzzle

Perfect for companies in chapter 11, hides losses while amusing shareholders. Our clever staff of wordsmiths finesses your difficulties into a series of horizontal and vertical puzzles. Pass them out at annual meetings with no. 2 pencils and duck embarrassing questions. Glossy or tattered stock to suit projected image. Also available: Quarterly Earnings Jigsaw Puzzle, Rubik's Report. SKU **CROSS**

M E M O

To: All Staff
From: The Poobah of Permanent Markers
Subject: Behavior at Recent Trade Show

Staff:

It has come to my attention that there were several instances of ugly and disgraceful behavior directed at employees of our rival, OfficeHacks, at last week's Upper Duluth Annual Office Supplies and Small Farm Animals Trade Show. I want all of you to publicly compose yourselves and always behave as proud Stooples employees should. To that end, below are a few corporate guidelines on acceptable decorum. Please take them onboard immediately:

1. When you see OfficeHacks staff on the floor of a trade fair, remember, you are the Big Dog. Growl if they approach your booth, as though they are the horrible schnauzer from down the block. Let your ears and hair rise menacingly; wag your tail with great vigor. If they come closer, bark loudly, then run from one end of the booth to the other. When they go away, drink some water from your dish and congratulate yourself on a job well-done.

2. If you catch them alone in the elevator, pull their shirts up over their heads hockey-style and pummel them mercilessly, flailing away until the refs or other elevator passengers come to their aid. Accept your "five-minutes-for-fighting" penalty gracefully, then skate quickly to the Stooples bench. Glare at them for the full five minutes. Remember to pick up your teeth.

3. Never urinate in their gas tanks. That is unseemly. Instead, pay the man at the nearby service station $10 to do it for you.

4. If you have a sexually transmittable disease, sleep with as many OfficeHacks employees as possible. Penicillin is always available after the show.

5. United we stand, fired you fall. Always cover the backs of your coworkers in any confrontational situation. If a parking-lot fight breaks out, gang-tackle, pinch, and give painful hickeys to the nearest OfficeHacks employee. It is important to show solidarity, even in a police lineup.

6. Remember, you are a child of the Universe; you have a right to be at the Upper Duluth Annual Office Supplies and Small Farm Animals Trade Show. And whether or not it is clear to you, no doubt the trade show is unfolding as it should. Therefore, be at peace with Stooples, whatever you conceive It to be.   With all its sham, drudgery, and broken dreams, it is still a beautiful business.

Regards,

Donny

Yawn Tie

Oversized bow tie lets you turn your head and yawn during meetings without fear of reprisal. Don't wish it known that the seminar is as engrossing as a test of the Emergency Broadcast System? Turn and yawn away! Also, blow bubbles, floss, gargle or even pick out that disgusting piece of broccoli by your molar. Finally, public privacy can be yours! SKU **Dagwood**

ONLY
$13.99

Save $6

Reg. $19.99

Bill Gates' Swiss Bank Account Number

$9.99

...list of the richest ...d yes, ...of with ...umber. ...for your ...and for ...yrtle Beach, ...All this for an ...Number ...ss efficiency ...r money back.

Remind boss not to scratch nuts during presentation.

LOW PRICE $1 **EACH**

Traveler's Chicks

Government-backed poultry is perfect for trade with Third World and Eastern European countries. Young fowls can be exchanged for lodging or office space and are especially valued in nations ravaged by famine or McDonald's. All USDA-approved, these birds are legal tender. Don't fly the coop without them. SKU **CHEEP**

Executive Burial Ashtray

Honor years of service. Stainless steel burial urns allow the interment of cremated remains right outside an executive's old office. Push-button office lobby-style ashtrays encourage open viewing by mourners and admirers. A real morale builder, gives the living something for which to strive. SKU **ASHES**

Walter J. Windgate

PRESS TO VIEW

Only $18⁹⁹

WE'RE PLEASED TO ANNOUNCE

Takeover $5⁰⁰ Announcement Cards

It pays to be polite. Ornate cards and envelopes take the sting out of unfriendly merger attempts; let you wreak havoc without losing your manners. Tasteful design will please lawyers, CEOs and the SEC (Stylish Exchange Commission). Choose from Sneak Attack Silver or Blitzkrieg Blue. SKU **SNAG**

Stooples T-Shirt

Stooples fashionable T-shirts, only $9.99, plus sales tax, shipping, FedEx man eats his lunch in a truck tax, "Where the hell did the receptionist put this?" finders fee, "Ow shit, I cut myself on the 'effing' scissors" tax, Band-Aid tax, clean the blood off the scissors tax, communicable disease alert tax, quarantine the whole goddamned office tax and "Oh, God, when it will it all end," overreacting surcharge. Specify S, M, S&M, M&M, Eminem, XL, XXL, Salad Bar Candidate.

Bail-Out Bucket

Keep your company above water with government-subsidized pail. Deep-set riveted bottom lets you fill it with mucho dinero; sturdy handle lets you carry it to and from federal coffers. Recommended by American Airlines, Argentina and lending institutions across America. Colors: In the Red, and Mint Green. SKU **BAIL**

$17⁹⁹

$67⁰⁰
Per Pair

Elevator Spring Shoes

People are still getting out of the elevator, but you've got to get inside before those other morons. Now you can! Elevator Spring Shoes let you catapult over the crowd even before they exit the elevator doors; lets you capture your favorite corner before it gets taken. Doors still shut? No problem! Built-in Demagnetizer opens locked doors even before the elevator arrives, gives you a chance for a running start. Hey, it's five o'clock—you have a life, too! SKU **JUMPY**

Logo Tattoo

You love tattoos (and who doesn't). But are you aware that when your pants slide down and you lean forward in your chair, your boss may have mixed emotions about seeing your posterior, your thong and a tattoo that says "Kill Authority"?

Ensure you don't lose executive goodwill over bodily expressions with Cover-Up Logo Tattoos. Bold company insignia on your behind shows higher-ups that the company sits well with you. Washable, removable, in case you ever decide to buy a belt. SKU **KILL AUTHORITY?**

$3⁹⁹

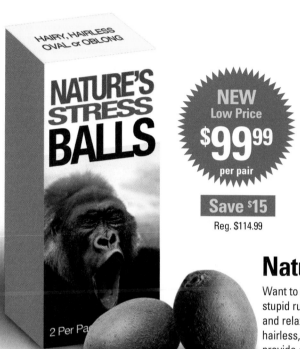

NEW
Low Price
$99⁹⁹
per pair

Save $15
Reg. $114.99

Nature's Stress Balls

Want to relieve stress at your desk but getting no satisfaction from that stupid rubber thing? Recycled gorilla testicles reduce worry, promote rest and relaxation by getting you directly in touch with nature. Hairy or hairless, oval or oblong, Nature's Stress Balls come two to a package and provide a strangely satisfying feeling that, somehow, in some way, you have gained control of a situation. Also available: Lion Balls, Tiger Balls and the balls of former Chrysler executives. SKU **BALL FOR $99 PER PAIR**

From our
"Shut Up Dog" Collection

Mechanical Rabbit

Home office workers, this is for you. Does your neighbor's dog bark six hours out of every day, interrupting phone calls, strategic thinking, two o'clock nap? Lifelike mechanical rabbit caroms around perimeter of neighbor's yard, incites barking dog until dog has massive heart attack. Perfect for yippy chihuahuas, growly basset hounds, incessantly grating cocker spaniels, etc. Not recommended for big dogs with long legs who can catch rabbit and eat it. SKU **LITTLE YIPPER**

ONLY
$85⁹⁹

"Try and catch us, you bonehead canine!"

Visit us online @ **www.stooples.com**

Call 1-800-STOOPLE

29

Letter from Your Stooples CFO, Julius D.W.I. de Krook

Dear Shareholders:

They don't call me "de Krook" for nothing. Fiscal 2004 was nothing short of a spectacular year. Not for you, unfortunately, but for your Stooples management team.

I'd like to take this chance to run you through some numbers: Had you invested $50 in our common stock last year, it would now be worth $50.13. Our top executives, on the other hand, exercised stock options that netted them tens of millions of dollars during the course of the year. It's all disclosed, grudgingly, and because it has to be, on page 1314A, section B, subsection 22, paragraph 4F, in the appendix of our annual earnings statement.

You may think Stooples is all about office supplies. But when you're a company with $220 million in revenue and fifteen hundred employees operating in highly competitive markets on three continents, diversification and active management of finances is critical. On that front, I can say modestly that you should be bowing down to me and doing the funky chicken because I was nothing short of brilliant in 2004.

Our number-one priority—as always—was to avoid taxes. We used a combination of inventory write-downs and aggressive accounting to ensure our tax bill stayed steady from a year earlier, despite a 23-percent jump in revenue.[1] If anyone who looks like a government representative asks, tell them that the pool table and corporate jet skis are for business purposes only.

Looking ahead, I feel pretty good about offshore vehicles, though I don't particularly like their gas mileage.

In terms of currency exposure, we ensured our delta never incurred any losses exceeding our alpha and beta underlyings. We were flexibly balanced across our dollar, yen, and euro positions to the point where our swaps, forwards, options, and warrants never fell into "death strike" territory. I can safely say our conservative hedges didn't need any major trimming.

What did require some trimming, though, was our budget. We hit a bit of a rough patch around midyear, forced to recall all of our 850,000 "Really Tight Clips" from global markets for safety reasons, after Johnny Larsen, a toddler in Aden, Utah, performed an unintended self-circumcision with a clip his father had stolen from the office. We settled with the boy's parents, admitting no fault, but man, did we have to shell out a bundle. Stooples promptly stopped buying toilet mints for the urinals in our men's bathrooms, rolled out a "Use That

Teabag Twice, You Wastrel" campaign, and started forcing our janitorial crew and their illegal alien families to sell our products door-to-door without commission or risk deportation.

Business Weak Magazine
See page 86

We emerged from that unfortunate, one-off incident stronger, smarter, and safer—and we can all rejoice in the knowledge that little Johnny's unplanned operation decreases his chances for penile cancer by 37.5 percent in his later years.

On the upside, I more than earned my base salary of $750,000, my $235,000 in options, and my $550,000 cash bonus in 2004. During the course of the year, I kept our acne-covered CEO (and I use that term loosely) from carrying out such harebrained schemes as a takeover of Hooters USA and merging it with Stooples under the motto "Stooples: Office Tools for Boobs." While we likely could have squeezed and tweaked some synergies out of such a T&A arrangement, it would have stretched us financially; and history suggests gravity would take over, causing our share price to eventually sag.

Looking ahead to 2005, you should feel confident that Stooples is being run by guys who know a thing or two about money management. Our intent is to learn one or two more things during the year, bringing our total to three or four by year-end.

My friends and fellow investors, it's probably appropriate to end with a quotation from Warren Buffett, the so-called "Sage of Omaha." A great man, a great friend, and a great customer of Stooples, he once told me, "I've got billions. I'm old and am gonna croak soon. The hell with bloodsucking investors. Give 'em crumbs and big speeches, and they'll be happy."

I promise lots of crumbs and big talk in the years to come.

Sincerely,

Julius D.W.I. de Krook

[1] Using the Black-Scholes-Weimar Republic method of valuing derivative instruments.
I have no idea what this all means.

Pre-Coupled Paper Clips

Ever notice how some paper clips are joined together while others lie loosely apart? Our guaranteed pre-coupled paper clips lie already linked in their box. Immediately useful as office necklace, metal lasso and thing to wave around so the boss sees you've been real productive for the last three years. Did we say they come already connected?
SKU **CLIP JOB**

$6⁹⁹ A BAG

S T O O P L E S   N O T E

Canadian Customers
Hey, you hockey heads, you've got to pay extra, eh? include Dominion tax, maple-syrup and round-bacon tax and the difference between your currency and real money.

Possess it for ONLY
$2,999⁹⁹

Demonic Computer Protector

Getting sucked into your computer is no way to build your business. New Demonic Computer Protector keeps you secure at your workstation and away from the forces of evil. Anti-sucking alert gives you ample time to hold on to your armrest when angry succubi try to pull your head into the terminal. Override button turns angry spirits into screen saver. Not effective against vampires or crazed serial killers who jump from the terminal and chase you around your office. SKU **BAD DAY**

WARNING!!!
Not effective against vampires or crazed serial killers!

demonic computer protector

Psychologically Engineered Office Chair

Every short, high-powered executive with a Napoleonic complex will love our power-lift psychologically engineered office chair. Negotiating with a 6'4" behemoth? One-touch button lifts you high over your adversary so you can look down on him for a change. Hydraulics are pleasantly muffled for a more subtle lift effect. Choose from three models: Shaq, Telephone Lineman, Godzilla. SKU **NOSE BLEED**

Don't forget who's the boss!

Save $20
$399⁹⁹
Reg. $419⁹⁹

"Memo Impossible" Cassettes

Sometimes it's just too hot to put on paper or e-mail. Spontaneously combustible cassettes are now available for interoffice use. Whether you're transmitting inside information or just passing along a sly innuendo, self-destructing tapes keep you from being identified as the source. Lets your secretary disavow any knowledge of your activities. Nontoxic smolder won't pollute.

SKU **GOOD** **$10**⁹⁹   SKU **LUCK** **$7**⁹⁹   SKU **JIM** **$4**⁹⁹

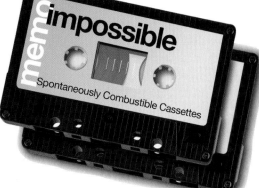

memo impossible
Spontaneously Combustible Cassettes

STOOPLES
Office Tools for Hopeless Fools

 Visit us online @ **www.stooples.com**

 Call 1-800-STOOPLE

Bird Poop Head Cone

Wide-mouth cone catches liquid before it hits, provides timely interference for scalp and shoulders. Leather headband holds cone in place, absorbs excess spillage. Empties easily into nearby shrubbery. SKU **DRIP**

Bolsha-Bic

Red-ink highlighter tells them who's in control. Aggressive marking fluid covers counterproductive words and phrases with a single stroke, spreads quickly to engulf entire paragraph. Great for purging revisionist leaders from the annual report or deleting digits from proletarian paychecks. Waterproof and NATO-proof. Also comes in Lenin Yellow, White Russian, People's Purple and Plain Old Pinko. SKU **NYET!**

ONLY $**19**¹⁷

Hands-On Desk Accessories

Nothing beats hands-on experience. Our friends at Qatar Office Supply now offer a limited supply of severed-hand desk accessories taken from limbs of convicted shoplifters and pickpockets. Experienced hands have large palms and lithe fingers for holding maximum quantities of desk supplies. Lay on side with closed fist for pen holding, lay flat with open palm for convenient ashtray. You'll think of thousands of other uses! A handy way to organize your desk! Also available from Tel Aviv Office Supply: Foreskin Briefcase! SKU **AAAIIEE!**

"Who Cut The Cheese?" Sodium Pentothal

It's only the middle of a meeting, but flatulence is a major problem. Just who cut the cheese? No one ever owns up, but you'll get answers quickly, thanks to Who Cut the Cheese Sodium Pentothal. Fast-acting serum gets them to admit it, fast. Great for eliciting confessions of Three Bean Lunches, Egg Salad Surprise and Cabbage Coq au Vin. Also prompts staff to admit who didn't wash hands after "health break." Wears off in five minutes, so you can begin lying to each other once more. Not available in Wisconsin. SKU **RIP ONE**

Only
$**32**⁹⁹

Flesh-Eating Zombie HR Dire...

Are you a collaborative or cooperative type?" "I hear you and under... your problems, b... things from the c... perspective." Wh... from your standar... type? Bring in a Fle... HR Director to deal ... personnel issues. Is ... harassing his 20-year-... again? Stop warning h... Flesh-Eating Zombie HR... Bob's lunch. No amount ... pleading, whining or sobb... through, no problems are ... to stop him from eating his ... through your staff troubles. ... never be the same. SKU **YUM**

Remember, I'm not fat, I'm growing with the company.

299⁹⁵

NEW
Low Price
$149⁹⁹

Hedge Against Inflation

Full-flowering shrubbery makes perfect addition to any investment portfolio. Tax-free growth won't soil long-range planning. Bushy asset branches out to cover more of your financial base. Place in blue-chip atrium or along fence to keep others from watching you count your money. SKU **GREENZ**

Back Patter

Now you can receive positive reinforcement even when your mentor is away. Motorized shoulder harness connects to two cushiony palms, delivers pat-after-pat pleasure following successful completion of assignments. Repertoire also includes hearty handshakes and a pinch on the cheek. SKU **GOODJOB**

ONLY
$39⁹⁹

$5^{99}
Box of 100

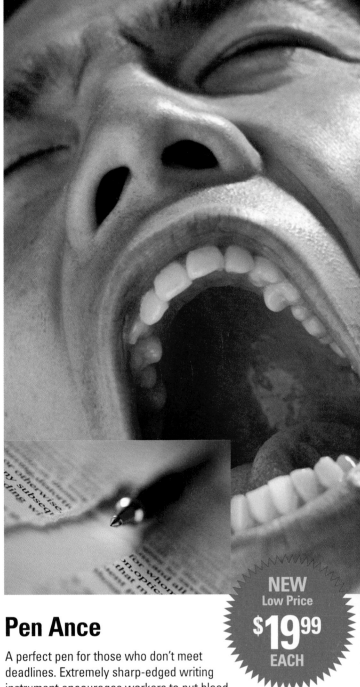

R.O.I Birthday Cards

Every birthday will now be greeted with return-on-investment notes that show they care—about what they get back. From your mom: "Happy birthday! Where's my kiss?" From your assistant: "Happy birthday, time to retire, lard-ass." From office custodian: "Happy birthday. I won't tell what I found in your garbage can for only $50 a week. You'll be so overwhelmed you'll wish your birthday occurred every day, that day being February 29th." SKU **SWEET NOTHINGS**

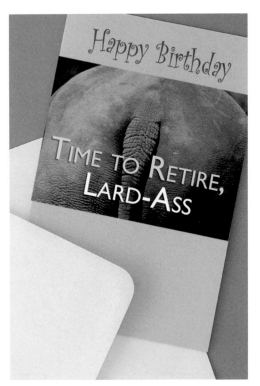

NEW
Low Price
$19^{99}
EACH

Pen Ance

A perfect pen for those who don't meet deadlines. Extremely sharp-edged writing instrument encourages workers to put blood, sweat and tears into every assignment. Acidic-based ink leaves burning impressions on reports, diagrams and very quick notes. Really smelly pen cap is rotten cheese and your grandmother's shoes rolled into one. Morale booster—not! SKU **PAINFUL**

M E M O

To: All Staff
From: The King of Cubicles, Donny Steintrumper
Re: Spurious federal allegations

I'm fully aware of the allegations of anticompetitive behavior leveled against us by our rival, OfficeHacks, in federal court. I'm writing to you today to assure you that all of them are spurious, and that we intend to vigorously contest them and expect to prevail. Specifically,

Our Corporate Espionage Team will swear under oath that they have absolutely no idea why they were arrested inside the OfficeHacks main product warehouse in Secaucus. They also advise that the stamps and labels marked "made cheaply in Kazakhstan using child labor" were planted by jealous competitors hoping to besmirch the great Stooples name.

Employees in our Rapid Reaction Team completely and utterly deny they disrupted the OfficeHacks annual general meeting by coughing "bullshit" every time one of the OfficeHack directors made a statement. Furthermore, they say there's no truth at all to the allegation that, as the lawsuit alleges, they "caused havoc and mayhem at the same meeting by shouting 'Food fight!' and throwing cold-cut slices, Swedish meatballs, and gobs of flan at various OfficeHacks shareholders and staff."

The manager of our flagship Newark store says he had nothing to do with setting up a roadblock some fifty feet from the entrance of a rival OfficeHacks store. He furthermore says he doesn't know who attached signs to the sawhorses that read, "OfficeHacks closed for bankruptcy proceedings. Shop at Stooples store 150 yards away at 1715 S. Elm."

My fellow Stooples staff, I want to emphasize that we not only welcome competition, we embrace it, even fondle it when no one's looking. On top of that, we respect all of our competitors, big and small, even when they're snotty crybabies who wear ladies' panties, though I'm not mentioning any names. Remember in the months ahead, as we plead our case in a court of justice, that truth is the ultimate defense.

Onward and upward,

Donny

Corporate Microwave Surprise

Forgot your lunch? A little light in the wallet before payday? No worries! Corporate Microwave Surprise lets you gather remnants of other people's dishes for a tasty treat that will satisfy any hunger. Comes with scraper, special sauce, antibiotic food coloring and certificate—exempting company management from OSHA fines and class-action lawsuits. Nothing to drink? Try Coffee Machine Surprise. Not available in countries monitored by the World Health Organization. SKU **TASTY!**

NEW $11⁹⁹

Corporate Microwave
SURPRISE
includes scraper, special sauce and antibiotic food coloring

Stripe On

Surprise meeting catch you in a humdrum suit? Thin-brush applicator lets you add classic pinstripes to stodgy attire in a matter of minutes. Add stripes to jacket, vest even shoes! Plaid? No problem! Add a quick coat of horizontal stripes. Machine wash to restore natural drear. SKU **SNAZ**

All Time Low $3⁹⁹

 STOøPLES
Office Tools for Hopeless Fools

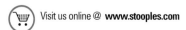 Visit us online @ **www.stooples.com**

 Call 1-800-STOOPLE

Personal Jingle

It works for advertisers, now let it work for you. Upbeat little tune can be played before salary reviews, speeches, etc. Personalized to promote both you and your accomplishments: "Miller is the man for you; he cut company losses in two!" Specify solo or choral. SKU **TA-DUM**!

Save $5
$24.99
Reg. $29.99

Call 1-800-STOOPLE
24 Hours/Day. 7 Days/Week.

or 1-800-HOT-CSRS
when you realize that none of these products are really for sale and you're just feeling naughty!

Boss's Daughter Neuter Spray

$39⁹⁹

Your boss's daughter lords it over you like you're a serf from the Middle Ages or a Smurf from the middle eighties. Now it's time to take a stand so future generations don't suffer the same fate. Boss's Daughter Neuter Spray superenhances performance of existing birth-control methods), reducing the odds that the boss's grandson will torture your children in 2031. Odorless and colorless, won't stain their clothes, unless you want it to. A great way to end the tyranny of nepotism! SKU **DADDY!**

Also Available!

Boss's Child Fertility Spray

You love your boss, and his kid is even better. Maximize the influence of this paternalistic crew with Boss's CHILD Fertility Spray. Triplets, quadruplets, wonderful future bosses will be birthing by the bushel! Will even work on the boss's husband/wife, mother and grandmother! A boon to future generations, unless of course the family sells the company. SKU **GRANDMOTHER?**

Edible Penties

When you chew your pen, does the taste of plastic leave you limp? Tasty, ultrafrilly penties dissolve in your mouth, not in your hands. Not in the mood? Slide-off action lets you remove penties, get down to business immediately. See-through barrel lets you know when it's time to refill. Flavors: Lost Cherry, Vanilla Moon, Double Moon Chocolate. SKU **PANT**

Coconut Caddy

Put the pen in the coconut, get yourself together. Put the pen in the coconut, then you'll feel better. Put the pen in the coconut, drink it all up. Put the pen in the coconut, then call me in the morning.
SKU **OOOH WOO**

$1
3 for

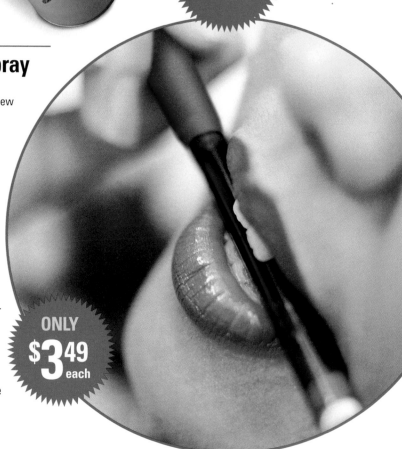

ONLY
$3⁴⁹
each

LOL Enhancer

Why is it that when people put LOL (laughing out loud) in their e-mail, it's never close to funny? LOL Enhancer adds much-needed humor to really lame LOL usage. Before use of LOL Enhancer: "Gee, I hate long meetings, let's try smoke signals." LOL. With application of LOL Enhancer: Cannibal: "Gee, I hate my mother-in-law." Other Cannibal: "So try the potatoes." LOL. Versions include Dry, Wry, Droll, Wayans Brothers, Marx Brothers, Bush Brothers, others.

SKU **YOU UNFUNNY MORON**

Stooples Quality Control

"Quality control is a Stooples hallmark. Every delivery is lovingly hand packed, and we guarantee you won't find a single pubic hair in your shipment. Ever."

Dividend Pelts

Bad quarter? Don't cut the dividend. Furry beaver pelts let you offer return on investment in fashionable early American style. Stacks of 150 pelts can be hauled to shareholder homes by a realistic dog team and old Yukon sled or by herniated UPS man. Also available: Dividend wampum.

SKU **DON'T SPEND THEM ALL IN ONE PLACE**

"MIRROR, MIRROR..."

NEW!

Talk-a-Mile

Talk too much at meetings? Precision pedometer attaches to neck, measures Adam's apple movement to gauge verbal mileage. Wafer-thin plating prevents bulging under necktie, lets you monitor in complete privacy. Appropriate for formal presentations or those quiet moments of talking to yourself. SKU **YAPPR** **$7**⁹⁹

$7⁹⁹

Career-Counseling Mirror

It's great to talk about career moves, but whom can you trust? Our Career-Counseling Mirror can help. Trustworthy mirror tells you what to do as long as you ask in rhyme (e.g., "Mirror, mirror, on the wall, should I stay or should I stall?"). Won't blab to snoopy HR types. Golden frame gives it a nice enchanted touch. SKU **S. WHITE**

$49⁹⁹

  Visit us online @ **www.stooples.com**  Call 1-800-STOOPLE

Chia Boss

When you take a two-week cruise to a Polynesian Paradise, what are your employees doing? Keep them from sleeping, shopping, smoking dope, joining organized religions and god knows what else with a lifelike Chia Boss. Just water days before you leave, place on desk and your employees will think you've never left (especially the nearsighted ones). Chia Boss is most effective when you are a short, hairy man with a head like a coconut. Never worry about productivity breakdowns again!

SKU **CHIA LATER**

All-Time Low

$**19**⁹⁵

FREE Watering Can
with every Chia Boss
purchase

Kama Sutra PDA

You love your PDA, don't you. Nestling in your office, scratching little addresses, scribbling little messages with a tiny penlike thing. Oh, so intimate. Now, Kama Sutra PDA can help you increase the level of intimacy you and your pocket toy share. Based on the suggestions of many pocket-sized computer observers, Kama Sutra PDA contains illustrated, sensual diagrams of the many body cavities in which you may place your digital organizer and in which public places it would be most appreciated. The marriage of love and technology has officially begun! SKU **WIDER**

$**79**⁹⁹

Spotlight Grabber

Make sure your accomplishments are noticed. Portable spotlight attaches to waist, rises three feet over head for dramatic effect. Includes bottle of SPF 10 sunscreen for bald or hair-challenged executives. SKU **TA DA!**

HOT ITEM
$58⁹⁹

NOW ONLY
$149⁹⁹

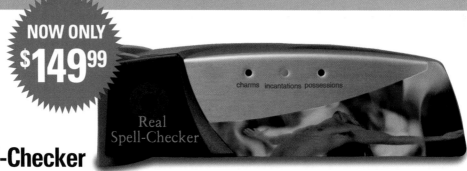

charms incantations possessions

Real
Spell-Checker

Save $20
Reg. $169.99

Real Spell-Checker

Ensure that your words are not only spelled correctly but remain free from the influence of charms, incantations and demonic possession. Lightweight, portable talisman fits on the back of any computer terminal, ensures that "Very Truly Yours" does not turn into "Up Yours" when you're not looking. Comes in Pure Red, Amulet Amber and Linda Blair Brown. Money back if terminal does a 360° on its stand or spews vomit on your coworkers. SKU **ENCHANTING**

46

Collection Bricks

No need to be subtle with deadbeats. Collection bricks mean no letters to write, no hassles on the phone. Four sizes of sturdy bricks can be thrown through cheapskates' windows: half a brick for week one to full-sized cinder block for week four. Approved by Manny, Danny and the entire gang at the Bayonne Social Club. SKU **THICK AS**

OUR LOWEST PRICE
$39⁹⁹
per set

Donald Trump's Hairnet $6⁹⁹

Box of 5

Buy for mother before she goes into home.

...ce. For a coiffure ... and maybe ...d's," try Donald ...efore you go to ...deal with ...webbing even ...because, yes, ...A and health ...s. Donald ...anywhere!

Podium Security Blanket

Save $1

$10⁹⁹

Reg. $11..99

Sturdy wool blanket absorbs palm sweat, fits comfortably on any lectern. If you bomb, throw over your head for instant anonymity. Place between knees to prevent knocking. Double-stitched pocket holds cue cards, crib sheets, selected cordials. SKU **CLUTCH**

STOOPLES
Office Tools for Hopeless Fools

M E M O

To: All Managers
From: The Prince of Pocket Protectors
RE: Budget cuts

All:

My father once told me something that has stuck in my head ever since. We were on a fishing trip, sitting in a boat in the middle of a big lake. It was 6 a.m. and we were going to be out there until at least 5 p.m., with only a couple of sandwiches and a bottle of water. I was really hungry, so I picked up a sandwich. "Son," he said. "You eat that sandwich now, and all you'll have left in the afternoon is sushi."

I tell you this because it's 6 a.m. in our budget year, and you've eaten way too many of my sandwiches. It's June, and you're already 17 percent ahead of budget. I don't want to hit any panic buttons here, but after putting my head together with our resident tightfist, CFO Julius de Krook, we realize your free-spending means that come November 1, you'll be looking to buy some water jugs for the cooler or to send Ed in accounting to the Houston office. And you know what? You won't be able to find a freaking dime.

Two words, ladies and gentlemen: Cut Costs! Do it yourself and get your staff to do it, too.

But let's also go a step farther and play with everyone's heads. We don't want staff to just not spend that extra dollar. We want them to feel guilty about even thinking about wanting to spend it. To that end, I give you "Operation Jewish Mother," a guilt-inducing, cost-savings plan you will roll out in the coming days and weeks, vastly changing our corporate culture.

1) Toilet Supplies: With immediate effect, please cut your paper towel and toilet tissue expenditures in half and switch to single ply from double ply. Don't say anything to staff. Let them wonder, as they sit there staring at a roll of toilet paper with just three measly sheets left, whether THEY were the ones who wasted all the toilet paper by wrapping and rolling a wad, instead of daintily patting with a piece or two. Or better yet, start leaving around last year's Stooples catalog in the stalls. Please also stop purchasing toilet mints for the urinals. They're a luxury.

2) Kitchens: I know that caffeine increases energy and productivity, but our expenses on coffee and tea bags are exorbitant. Please post "signs" prominently in every kitchen that read, SHARE A TEA BAG WITH YOUR FRIENDS and COFFEE SO GOOD I MADE A SECOND POT WITH THE SAME FILTER AND GROUNDS! Our goal is to have every coffee filter and grounds used for two pots, and tea bags used for at least three cups of tea. After all, coffee is coffee and tea is tea, no matter how many times you run the water through them, right?

3) Mileage Reimbursements: We currently reimburse at nine cents a mile for our salespeople, who travel around the country to sell our great products. That will not change. However, I've instructed the security guards in our parking lots to assist us in our cost-cutting efforts by waiting until our salespeople have returned their cars to the parking lot and reentered the building and then turning back their odometers. As managers, you'll start to notice discrepancies, which you will attribute to cheating by sales staff. For that, please sternly rebuke them, threaten them with job loss if it happens again, and readjust their mileage forms to reflect the "real" mileage traveled.

I estimate these three measures alone will cut 22 percent from our budget by end-August, with full-year savings of 28 percent. I also welcome any and all other spending cuts you want to introduce, provided none of them are attributed to me. I also promise a bonus of $2,500 and a trophy inscribed MISERLY BASTARD OF THE YEAR for the most innovative and painful spending cut you're able to push through.

Regards,

Donny

Holographic VIPs

Go one better than name-dropping. Three-dimensional images of top business leaders sitting in your office show that you're really in conference. Holographic figures speak and move like actual counterparts, drink holographic coffee, flick holographic ashes on carpeting. Bill Gates, Alan Greenspan, Mr. Peanut. Others available on request. SKU **3D**

STOOPLES PRICING POLICY

Prices in our Stooples Catalog are often theoretical and can be changed without notice depending on cash flow, mood or time of the month. If we are Grumpy, expect a 4% grumpy tax. If we are Dopey, please add an additional 5% and if we are Doc, 10% on top of that, but only with the proper HMO codes.

 Visit us online @ **www.stooples.com**

 Call **1-800-STOOPLE**

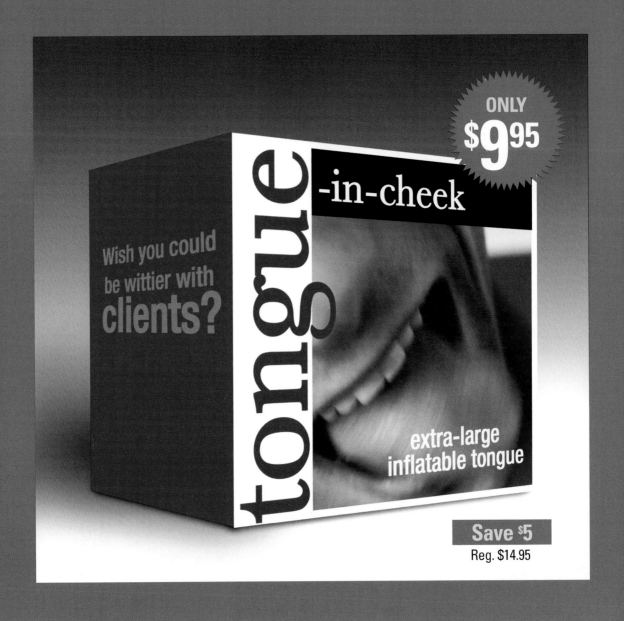

Tongue-in-Cheek

Wish you could be wittier with clients, a master of repartee at office Christmas parties? Extra-large, inflatable Tongue-in-Cheek provides mouthfuls of charm and waggish wit at even the stuffiest of occasions. Deliver bon mots with amusing regularity even if you don't know a bon mot from a bladder infection. Japes, jokes and quips galore! Specify model: Mark Twain, Will Rogers, Chris Rock or Terry, the Toitty-Mouthed Transsexual. SKU **IN JEST**

50

 Visit us online @ **www.stooples.com**

 Call 1-800-STOOPLE

Yes-Man

A good yes-man is hard to find! Bobbing-head doll in three-piece suit does wonders for the ego in search of massage. Spring-action neck promotes total agreement with inane suggestions, unbridled enthusiasm for half-baked schemes. Hand-painted, obsequious smile tells you you're the greatest! SKU **YESJB**

UNBEATABLE PRICE
$8 99

BIODEGRADEABLE

ONLY
14¢
each

Number Two Pen Holder

Somewhat solid, all-natural pen holder solves the age-old dilemma of "waste not, want not." Perfect for those companies on an extreme cost-cutting frenzy. When your CFO brings up Spend Management, show him this (Caution: use of latex gloves highly recommended). Colors: Don't Ask.
SKU **SECOND TIME ROUND**

CEO Sodomizer $29 99

You thin
compan
paltry ra
Release
rage at t
wage. CE
boss dee
way up to
in and ou
and just e
offending
"bitch." W
promotion
SKU **SODEEP**

Who wants this?! Lobotomy Patients Gone Wild?

Panic Mutton

Overstuffed lamb doll cuddles close during times of crisis. Soft woolen curls nuzzle cheeks, resist rending and biting. Deep brown eyes offer love even when you're an abject failure. Deluxe talking mutton agrees that he's a "baaaaaaaaad boss" when you rub belly fleece.
SKU **BAA-BAA**

$**18**⁹⁹

"Baaaaaaaaaad Boss"

NOW ONLY
$**39**⁹⁹

Counteroffensive Refrigerator Signs

Many home-office employees spend as much time at their refrigerator as they do at their desks. Counteroffensive Refrigerator Signs encourage them to have an apple rather than the six-pound bowl of rice pudding their wife made for the family reunion. Subtle motivating signs include "Get Away from Me, Mr. Size 47," and "Do You Know the Price for Two First-Class Airplane Tickets Just for Your Butt?" Not recommended for female home workers who may find signs offensive and take it out on Mr. Size 47 when he gets home.
SKU **AN APPLE, IT'S TASTY, REALLY!**

"Is that a bowling ball in your shirt, or you just happy to see me?"

ONLY $**6**⁹⁹

"Go ahead, keep eatin', you *fat bastard!*"

Accent Decoder

It sounds like English, but what the hell are they saying? Don't let heavy accents scramble important phone messages. Electronic decoder makes southerners, New Yorkers and other foreigners sound as though they actually live here. Attaches easily to mouthpiece, resists tampering and ethnic abuse. SKU **WHAT?**

52

 STOOPLES Office Tools for Hopeless Fools

 Visit us online @ **www.stooples.com**

 Call 1-800-STOOPLE

Cult of Personality Photos

Your employees may respect you, but do they revere you? Spectacular 110' x 140' outdoor photo can go a long way toward convincing them of your divine leadership. Airbrushing puts benevolent twinkle in your eyes, gives you sad, knowing smile to remind them of your love. Angelic blue backdrop provides aura of heavenly approval. Hang from roof of headquarters or staple to bridge on way to work. SKU **MAO**

ONLY
$5.99

$299.99

Get your career on the

Fast-Track

Hey Whitey Correction Fluid

You still see him everywhere. He's comfortable in the halls of power as well as the golf course, but never at an Al Sharpton fund-raiser. He's kind of pale, thinks "Play that Funky Music, White Boy" is a compliment and is still trying to figure out how to make a move on his 24-year-old assistant without being fired, divorced and simultaneously laughed at by the 24-year-old. But somehow, through the years, he's still in demand. Now he has his own designer correction fluid. Isn't it about time? Hey Whitey: Distinctively You. SKU **HONKEYCAT**

Fast-Track Disposable Razor

The razor for the executive on the move lets you shave quickly between promotions. Smoothes rough spots before taking on sideburns or other assignments. Balanced "Handle on the Situation" gives you much-needed grip. Lady Fast-Track available for getting a leg up on the competition. SKU **NUBS**

Save $2

$5.99

Reg. $7..99

Includes

"Thanks for nothing"
engraving on stem

Low Price
$99.99
Reg. $125.99

Retirement Gourd

Why give a gold watch for 30 years of loyal service when the lazy SOB probably couldn't find another job anyway? Retirement Gourd is good enough for a career that stalled early and often. You want to give a gold watch to someone? Give it to the guy who worked seven jobs in six years and still has people begging to hire him. I mean, what's that about? He'll tell you to take your gold watch and shove it where ...hey, put me down! Fired? Asshole!

SKU **GOOD-BYE**

  Visit us online @ **www.stooples.com**  Call 1-800-STOOPLE

NEW!!

Super E-Mail Extender

Your e-mail on supply-chain improvement is a thing of beauty, but are people really reading it? Super E-Mail Extender drops your text into the next 257 e-mails they receive, leaving many lasting impressions. Your words will be inserted into Web searches, spread sheets, porno sites, shopping excursions and games where President Bush gets hit with a banana. Also available: Super CC Extender, which will send your e-mail to NATO forces, terrorist groups and to women who won't date you because you are a pain in the ass.

SKU **INSERT HERE** **$8**⁹⁹   SKU **IEXTEND THIS** **$18**⁹⁹

AdVenture Capital

Enough with due diligence, PowerPoint presentations and months of negotiations. Who needs venture capital from those dreary Wall Street bankers? Now there's AdVenture Capital when your company needs start-up funds. This is financing the way it was meant to be. Every red cent in this pool was stolen, embezzled or needs to be laundered. After all, pirates, crooked executives and mafia capos need to invest, too. Why not let these devils provide your angel financing. Choose from plundered Spanish doubloons, stolen diamonds, derivatives from the Enron pension fund or the $3.6 million taken at gunpoint in the Newark airport heist. Free prospectus, if you dare! SKU **PLANK – A FREE PROSPECTUS IS FREE, YOU IDIOT**

ONLY $99⁹⁹

Please Note

All Stooples products are Homeland Security–approved, except for our Condoleeza Rice toilet paper and the desktop mini-missile launchers, which can be purchased only with cash through Haliburton companies.

Three-Hole Paper Borer

The first environmentally safe paper puncher. Specially trained bookworms chew in straight lines through reports and memos, bore up to four volumes at a sitting. No messy confetti leftovers—paper is munched, not punched. Self-propagating creatures ensure long product life. SKU **MUNCHY**

Save $2
$22⁹⁹
Reg. $24.99

The "Hold" Switcheroo

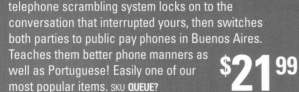

No one likes to be put on hold, especially you! Now you can strike back with the Switch Hold. Unique telephone scrambling system locks on to the conversation that interrupted yours, then switches both parties to public pay phones in Buenos Aires. Teaches them better phone manners as well as Portuguese! Easily one of our most popular items. SKU **QUEUE?**

$21⁹⁹

Typo Whip

Teach your secretary the value of proofreading. Woven strands of correction tape form foot-long whip; allow on-the-spot disciplinary action for forgetting to spell-check. Punish letter-dropping, reverse-wording and too much spacing. Horse-whip or cat-o'-nine-tails. SKU **OUCH**

NEW
Low Price
$29⁹⁹

Honor System Munchie Interrogrator

Who took the Twinkies and didn't pay for them? The cardboard-flavored chocolate cookies? Or even the cheese-filled crackers that taste of neither cheese nor crackers but still display attractive packaging? Honor System Munchie Interrogator analyzes emotional, cognitive and physiological speech patterns, then zaps the cheapskate who ate the gummy fish and didn't fess up. A great way to maintain inventory control and participate in corporate-sponsored S&M. SKU **TWINKIE TRUTH**

$**89**.95
Honest!

"I swear I didn't take the Twinkies!"

Lip Tightener

$**4**.99
each

Nondisclosure agreements are never enough! Lip balm ensures secrecy during sensitive negotiations, "quiet periods" and the moments before merger or "uh-oh, we've missed analyst expectations big-time" announcements. Really, really approved by the SEC and Nervous Nellie CFOs everywhere. SKU **PUCKER**

Lip Tightener

LOW-CARB PACKAGING

For pica sufferers, Stooples offers the industry's only low-carb, ingestible packaging materials. From Styrofoam peanuts to edible Bubble Wrap, Stooples packaging materials make for some good eatin'. They're 10% nontoxic and won't make you fat. And if you like what's inside, take a bite out of the box, itself. Mmmmmm.

Nasduq

Veritable quacky thing much safer investment than crazy high-tech exchange. Bad news and water roll off feathers with barely a ripple. Web feet know where the bottom is. Sharp duck bill investigates plankton and phony financial practices better than creepy conflict-of-interest, Big Six accounting firms. Much cuter than AFLAC duck. Specify Yellow or Ray of Sunshine. SKU **QUACK QUACK**

Save $30
**$89**^{99}
Reg. S119.99

STOOPLES Office Tools for Hopeless Fools

Visit us online @ **www.stooples.com**

Call **1-800-STOOPLE**

Mood Lectern

Don't just give a speech; tell them what mood you're in. Mood-alerting lectern has front panel that changes color with changes in your disposition. "Ungrateful louts who have abandoned us in our time of need!"—fiery red with flashes of burnt orange. "More bonuses, stock options and free gummy fish for everybody!"—aqua blue with rolling waves of Ben Franklin green. Not effective before the National Association of the Blind. SKU **PEACE**

GREAT PRICE
$349⁹⁹

FREE
Stooples Coffee Mug

with a purchase of $4,000 or more of Stooples merchandise. Mug is also available in Sucker Yellow.

Sales & Motivation Book Closeout

Our sales-training manuals have motivated thousands of salesmen to go back to school and become computer programmers and hairdressers. So it's best we get rid of these books as quickly as possible:

- The Story of Old Four Toes —turn-of-the-century salesman tells of his experiences getting a foot in the door.
- Winning Through Recrimination —sometimes self-pity can make people buy because they feel sorry for you and want you out of their house.
- The Greatest Used Belly-Button Lint Salesman in the World—areally disgusting book you should send to salespeople at other companies.

SKU **TAKE THEM ALL, PLEASE**

Other Titles:
- Think Big and Make Millions
- Think Bigger and Make Billions
- Close the Sale Already, A**hole
- Eleven Secrets of Selling to Lobotomy Patients

ONIY
$1⁴⁹
Per Set

NEW
Low Price
$19³²

Great Depression Wall Mural

Remind your employees who really controls the means of production. Vibrant, easy-to-install wall mural depicts scenes of severe economic hardship. Apple vendors and soup kitchens sharply contoured for maximum impact. Socialist realism on 50-pound straw-gray stock. Guaranteed to increase productivity by 200%! Not available in Silicon Valley. SKU **HOOV**

 STOOPLES
Office Tools for Hopeless Fools

 Visit us online @ **www.stooples.com**

 Call 1-800-STOOPLE

Czech in the Mail

Need to forestall payments but hate to lie to creditors? Unemployed Czech artist Miloslav Dvorak will don official U.S. postal bag, sit in mailroom for hours at a time while you happily call banks, suppliers, Mom or whomever else you owe money. Now you can truly say, "The Czech is in the mail!" Will also paint incomprehensible murals of Czechs suffering under Soviet rule, nude portraits of Janet Reno or whatever your mail crew desires! Hungary for alternatives? Budapest sculptor Istvan Kovalovszki will turn Pitney Bowes machine into flower pot, DVD player or a sculpture of General Grant falling off a horse. SKU **CZECH MATE**

$125 per hour

Subliminal Rushing-Water Meeting Excuser

They're still not getting up? Execute the health-break maneuver with Subliminal Rushing-Water Meeting Excuser. They won't know why, but when you see chairs shifting, knees bouncing and lips biting, end the meeting quickly and get out of the way! Not recommended for companies with fewer than five stalls per floor. SKU **FLOOD**

  Visit us online @ **www.stooples.com**  Call 1-800-STOOPLE

"I'm switching over to Conference-Call Sense-Maker before that jackass loses the account!"

ONLY $24⁹⁵

Conference-Call Sense-Maker

NEW There's always one person in a conference call who's a few bricks short of a load. Conference-Call Sense-Maker allows you to simulate the voice quality of the village idiot, end their connection and then take over their part of the conference call as you simultaneously continue your own. Use second-voice projection to gain agreement for your own proposals ("Helluva idea, Jim.") while also blasting opponent's theories ("What an idiot you are, Bill. Thank God Jim has good ideas."). Should be used with caution if Bill is bigger than Jim.

SKU **YOU DA MAN**

 STOOPLES Office Tools for Hopeless Fools

 Visit us online @ **www.stooples.com**

 Call **1-800-STOOPLE**

Paisley Remover

Paisleys are nice, but don't let them run amuck on your clothing. Executive-strength cleaner removes amoebalike patterns before they reproduce. Spray on infested garments; within minutes, lifeless paisleys will fall to the floor. Won't harm stripes, monograms or family crests. SKU **NO PAIZ**

BEFORE

NOW
$**4**99

One Spray Does The Trick

AFTER

Pee Alert Cell Phone Sound Manipulator

Are you aghast when you're on a cell phone and the other party decides to multitask bathroom and work functions simultaneously? If you're like millions of people, you'll want to mask the sounds of irrigation with our Pee Alert Cell Phone Sound Manipulator. Let's say you're in midconversation and you hear the ominous zipper heading in the wrong direction. Pee Alert rushes into action, providing your aural pathways the alternatively refreshing sounds of the crash of waves at Malibu or a small tsunami destroying a Papua New Guinea village. Toilet flush the final indignity? Our Sound Manipulator launches classic melodies of "Bridge over Troubled Waters," "Many Rivers to Cross" and "Down by the Old Mill Stream." You'll both feel refreshed, and then back to the business at, uh, hand. SKU **NIAGARA** $**44**99

STOOPLES
Office Tools for Hopeless Fools

ORDER FORM

Visit us online @ **www.stooples.com**

Call 1-800-STOOPLE *24/7 Order Hotline* **Call Now.** Our operators are standing by. They are still standing by. Yep . . . . still standing by. Would you call for crissakes! They're getting tired from all the standing.

Last Name _____ First Name _____

MI, Embarrassing Prefix Suffix Dr., but not pretentious Ph.D. _____ Childhood Nickname (eg. "Spunky," "Liver Lips") _____

Age _____ Sex _____ Favorite Position _____ Boxers or Briefs _____

Address 1 _____

Address 2 _____

City _____ State _____ State of mind _____

Credit Card #1 _____ Credit Card #2 _____

Bank Acct # _____ Bank PIN Code _____ Burglar Alarm Code _____ Online Banking Password _____

Product#	Qty.	Price Ea.	Page#	Description	Total Price
					Shipping
					Total Order

What We Stand For Besides the National Anthem, Stooples stands for quality and low prices. Our products are guaranteed to be 100%. If you receive only 80%, we'll send the other 20% COD. Remember, at Stooples we stand behind our products. From a distance, you'll never even notice.

How to Order Online
Duhhhh! You'll need a computer and an Internet connection. You'll need to deactivate cookie protection and enable those annoying pop-up ads, spyware, adware, and any other ware. Go to www.stooples.com. Click on a product, put it in your Stooples shopping cart, and proceed to Checkout. Stooples keeps your personal data safe with a 2.65-bit encryption system from the mid-1980s that we bought from a bankrupt Hungarian technology company on eBay.

How to Order by Mail
Stamps are helpful, and envelopes, too. Use our order form or any other paperlike substance. Ask your mother to lick the gummy part of the envelope so you won't get icky all over your tongue.

How to Order by Telephone
Pick up and dial. We welcome your phone orders, but speak English when you call. We

don't do Swahili, Frog, Bean Picker, Fortune Cookie, or Camel Jockey, and we only accept DOLLARS, not dinars, rubles, forints, or anything else. Orders over $25 shipped free if you can remember the first two stanzas of our corporate song.

Canadian Customers
Hey, you hockey heads, you've got to pay extra, eh? Include Dominion tax, maple-syrup and round-bacon tax, and the difference between your currency and real money.

Overseas Customers
Stooples is happy to ship overseas when we can find a box. Orders ship by air. Not responsible for water damage if shipped by sea.

Stooples Mailing List
If your address label is incorrect or you're moving, please let us know. We net over 23 percent of our income through sales of your name to other catalogs, magazines, and draft boards. We appreciate your help in this matter.

Low-Price Guarantee
Stooples sells stuff to make money and prices accordingly. We're not the Salvation Army. If you ever spot a product elsewhere that's priced lower than what we offer, we suggest you buy it, because we're not a bazaar or flea market.

Damaged Goods
The product we shipped you worked when we sent it out. If it's chipped, broken, or otherwise not functioning as advertised, all we can say is "tough titties."

Return Policy
Unhappy with your widget or thingamajig? Well, boo-frigging-hoo! Return it to us within forty-eight hours for your money back, but only in person, on every second Tuesday of the month, between 1:30 p.m. and 2:30 p.m., to our customer service center in charming Omagh, Northern Ireland. Remember to wear our "I Don't Brake for Catholics" T-shirt.

39^{00}
per pair

EMPLOYMENT
LAWYER
350^{00}
per hour

Cross-Eyed Cleavage Deflector

Like to look at exposed cleavage but hate to appear un-PC? Creative eyewear shows your eyes looking in different directions even as you stare right at them! Will fool even the most lawsuit-happy employee, not to mention their attorneys and 87% of jurors! Warning: Not to be worn while driving a car or trying to walk in a straight line. SKU **CROSS-EYED GLASSES**

Tex Messaging

Get "wired" from your home on the range. Our stylish Tex Messaging–enabled mobile phone will have even the thickest cowpoke sending SMS in no time. Twenty-two preset messages for every occasion—and they even sound just like you. Dog died? Girlfriend left you for your best friend? Tex Messaging has you covered. Tell your compadres, "Shucks, did y'all see that set of bodacious ta-tas?" Use romantic pickup lines like "I'm fixin' ta mount my hoss, little filly. Wanna join me?" and much, much more. Includes protective case in either faux rattlesnake skin or hand-stitched bison leather. Optional loop fits saddle pommel or gun rack. Also available: Tet Messaging for Vietnam Veterans.
SKU **YEE-HAW**

Shee-it, did y'all see that set of bodacious ta-tas?

199^{99}
with Service Contract

STOOPLES
Office Tools for Hopeless Fools

Visit us online @ **www.stooples.com**

Call 1-800-STOOPLE

In minutes, the scum & residue disappear right before your eyes <u>or does it?</u>

3^{99}
Per Cup

NeverClean Coffee Cup

You know you hate to clean coffee cups. Why bother? NeverClean Coffee Cup keeps your coffee fresh and your immune system relatively intact. Never wash, but also never see mold, fungus, mildew or any other disgusting coffeetime residue. Our secret? Camouflage. No matter what goes on in there, our David Copperfield–approved coffee cup never shows the true story, leaving you to assume all is white and sparkly. Also available: NeverClean Plates, Computer Keyboards and Third Stall on the Right. SKU **NOLOOK**

CE-OAF

The annual meeting was almost a riot, and the fiscal picture would make a porn star blush. Need a scapegoat? CE-OAFs will shoulder responsibility for all your company's missteps, miscues and monumental disasters. Throw blame, insults, fruit…CE-OAF will shrug it off, go back to picking flies off hairy arms. Large misshapen executive won't harm shareholders' children or your company's turnaround effort. When finished, return CE-OAF to nearest cave until you need him again. Also available: CF-OAF, Carl the Dumbass Controller. SKU **MECEO**

399^{99}
Per Annual Meeting

Staple Repair Kit

Company on an economy drive? Show your support by hammering used staples until they're good as new. Three-piece kit includes miniature anvil, hammer and forge. Optional hay can be strewn around office for total blacksmith effect. A favorite of supply clerks everywhere. SKU **THONK**

NOW ONLY $18⁰⁰

Chinese Food Condiment Holder

These 20-ft cylinders will hold tens of thousands of unused packets of soy sauce, Chinese mustard, and sweet 'n' sour goo that come with every Chinese culinary experience. Easy-to-grasp condiment tongs firmly pick up packages left on cafeteria table and allow insertion into proper cylinder. Collected substances useful as pothole filler and copier machine lubricant, or just rub on CEO after a bad quarter.

SKU **AH SO**

$109⁹⁹ Per Cylinder

"Bitty" Model Holds Three Erasers Easily!

Dead-Bolt Eraser Safe

Convenient office protection. One-inch dead-bolt safe secures erasers, paper clips, buttons, even stamps. Heavy-gauge steel plating discourages hardened supply snatchers, withstands limited mortar attacks and squeezing between thighs. Special security tweezer allows easy manipulation of combination lock.

SKU **ITTY (1" MODEL)** **$35⁹⁹**

Rather Not

Pushy television reporter on your back for more information? Aerosol spray emits protective cloud to separate you from the cameras, tells Dan you'd "Rather Not." Plumelike cloud is nontoxic and nonpenetrable by light and sound. Eight-oz. can stops Sean Hannity midsentence, makes Brit Hume fume. SKU **NO TV** $6⁹⁹

Office Politics Folder

Is he just lazy or is he the boss's winy nephew from Nantucket? A quick peek at his Office Politics Folder will tell you whether to fire him or make him your second-in-command. Detailed folder records family connections, country club memberships and incidents of nepotism. Phrases questions according to current Social Register standards. Solves the question of elite or delete once and for all! SKU **IPULL**

$1⁴⁹
Pack of 10

Plastique Bathroom Explosive

BREATHE EASY
$79⁹⁹

How to put this delicately? Company bathrooms are often windowless and without sufficient ventilation. But often one can't afford to wait until the malodors disperse and the bouquet of "monkeys having a poop fight" dissipates. Plastique Bathroom Explosives allow you to quickly and efficiently blow a small 2' x 3' hole in the restroom wall, creating instant ventilation so you may reach the stall without passing out. Muffled detonation won't cause stir in surrounding offices or cubicles. Hole should be covered with framed photo of the board of directors to remove suspicion and remain available if you need it again. And you will. Department of Homeland Bathroom Security—approved! SKU **POOF**

M E M O

To: Heads of Sales & Marketing Departments
From: The Emperor of Erasers
Re: Keeping your jobs and our pricing strategy

All:

It has come to senior management's attention that we're spending tens of thousands of dollars a year trying to figure out how to price our items. People, I don't care if that's what they teach you at Harvard, Yale, or Wharton. At dear, old Pace University's night business program, we learned business is all about moving product, and recent figures show me we're not doing that. To that end, CFO de Krook and I want to roll out our new, more aggressive pricing plan. Let's call it "Operation Undercut."

Instead of pulling your chins and scratching your heads trying to work out to the penny what our logistics and infrastructure costs are, here's what I want you to do. When you quote a price to a retailer or wholesaler, casually ask what OfficeHacks is charging for the same item. If the price is lower than the one you quoted—say forty-seven cents per item, compared with your offer of fity cents each—cough twice, slap your forehead with your palm, and say, "Oh, did I say fity cents a unit? I meant forty-six cents, because you're such a good customer."

I know you all work on commission, based on the size of the sale you've made, so I understand your fears that shaving margins will also sharply reduce your commissions. That's why this memo is circulated on the same day that we've just introduced our new "Overpriced Executive Line," basically the same office-supply garbage we already sell, produced at the same places and for the same cost, just stuck in nicer gold-colored and silver-colored boxes with ribbons on them, designed to make executives feel important and willing to pay 40 percent more.

So be of good cheer and keep those expense accounts down. Go forth and sell, sell, sell!

Onward and upward,

Donny

Resumayonnaise

Company not taking your unsolicited résumé? We have the answer. Creamy smooth Headhunter's Resumayonnaise is perfect for HR conference rooms, company cafeterias and those little office refrigerators that are cleaned only once every three years. Spreads thick on cold cuts and condiments. Within seconds, your name and phone number will flow through bread slices to keep you top of mind, as well as over hands and fingers. When they investigate ingredients, there's your work history! Brings out the best in every meal and search for employment. Also available: CV Salad, "Will Work for Food" Fondue. SKU CREAMIN

$9.99 Each

Resumayonnaise

Creamy smooth Headhunter's Resumayonnaise is perfect for HR conference rooms, company cafeterias and those little office refrigerators that are cleaned only once every three years.

Janet Wylander

Temperature Control Meeting-Ender

You've made your decisions, but no one wants to get back to work. Temperature Control Meeting-Ender causes sudden rise or fall of conference room temperature so people will quickly remember their next appointment. Choose from Sahara, Ice Age or Really Damp Day in the Bronx. SKU HOTHOTHOT **$9.99**

Gym Away Deodorizer

One hour for lunch, but your exercise routine takes 58 minutes. No time for shower? Not a problem! Gym Away Deodorizer hides gym smells fast. Doesn't exactly get rid of the smell, but turns it into something more confusing that couldn't possibly be you. Choose from Frogs Mating on a Hot Day, Cops and Doughnuts and new Pie Fight with Clowns. Works up to 150 yards and two days of nonshowering. Third day? Seek professional help immediately. SKU PEEHOO

$10.99 a Bottle

71

Flavored Frames

Do you suck on the frames of your glasses when contemplating important business decisions? Our gourmet glasses stimulate your palate as you ponder options, strategies and luck. Lightly flavored frames can't be beat for tasty after-meeting analyses or a postmortem munch. Three exciting flavors will invigorate your taste buds: Rocky Road, Sour Grapes and Brill de Crème. Never settle for the taste of hair and dandruff again! SKU **FRAMZ**

NEW ITEM $20²⁰

Rolohex File

Effective business incantations are now only a fingertip away. Rolohex file holds charms, curses and oaths; separates according to potency and FDA guidelines. Swivel control makes it simple to bless an acquisition or turn competitors into bloodsucking zombies. Weighted amulet base protects against tampering by analysts, short sellers and demonic investors from the fourth dimension. SKU **ZAP!**

$13⁹⁹

Go Away Gavel $22⁹⁹

Add a little pomp and circumstance to every downsizing. Real walnut gavel is favorite of human resources directors who truly love their work. Special molded grip ensures you don't lose control and accidentally smack your about-to-be ex-employee, adding injury to insult. Special wooden base provides true "thwack, thwack" effect, letting everyone know that the employment is adjourned. SKU **ORDER!**

 Visit us online @ **www.stooples.com**

 Call 1-800-STOOPLE

Braille for the Hard of Hearing

Are you deaf, or
Braille for the Ha
answers that qu
for all. Hammer,
and Morse Code
ensure the hard-
your message, ev
read lips. Nothing
point more than c
forehead. Buy no
tap, tap your way
opportunity emplo

SKU **ANBODYHOME**

made in Bangludouche!

Holler Helper

Why yell your lungs out? Preprogrammed audio box screams for assistants and secretaries at the touch of a button, calls for as many as 15 subordinates at a time. A godsend during times of crisis and when you run out of coffee. Optional echo chamber motivates the sluggish and easily impressed.

SKU **HEYU**

Only $79⁹⁹

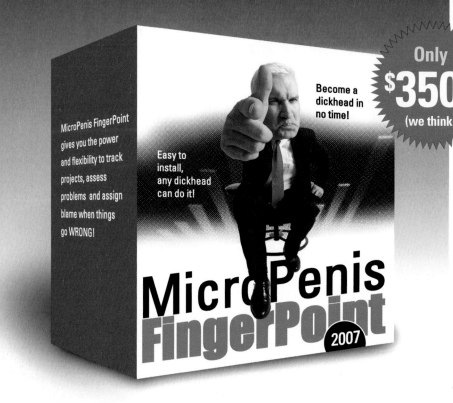

Only
$350⁹⁹
(we think)

ONLY
$**14,000,000**
per incursion

Become a
dickhead in
no time!

Easy to
install,
any dickhead
can do it!

MicroPenis FingerPoint gives you the power and flexibility to track projects, assess problems and assign blame when things go WRONG!

MicroPenis FingerPoint 2007

UNIPF

MicroPenis Project FingerPoint

MicroPenis Project FingerPoint gives you the power and flexibility to track projects, assess problems and assign blame when things go wrong. New Web-based collaboration project, CYACentral, lets everyone simultaneously identify scapegoats and report that they were at the doctor that day. Team building at its finest!. SKU NOTME

United Nations Interdepartmental Peacekeeping Force

Blue-helmeted forces, fresh from another Balkan adventure, are pleased to help you keep the peace between marketing, engineering, finance and other belligerent and unruly departments. Happy-faced soldiers from Fiji, Sweden and Nigeria can also separate opposing voting blocs at annual meetings, keep merged human-resource executives from each other's throats and whisk deposed CEOs away to a neutral third company. Includes photo op with UN secretary general and free ice cream from UN cafeteria. SKU KOFI

74

STOOPLES
Office Tools for Hopeless Fools

Visit us online @ **www.stooples.com**

 Call **1-800-STOOPLE**

Floppy Discus

Get more out of your software. Flexible CD-ROM provides reliable information storage, doubles as recreational device for use at company picnics. Shock-resistant, protects data during spins across field. Extra-thick oxide coating resists pizza stains and carnage by dogs and children. SKU **WHEEE**

ONLY
$**6**⁹⁹

Spin-Off Dreidl

Your subsidiaries are all turkeys, so which one should you spin off?

Our Spin-Off Dreidl makes it easy to decide. Dreidl sides list tottering subsidiaries—a quick flick of the wrist puts high-level decision making into motion! Spin for best two out of three if you're unhappy with the result. A real time-saver! SKU TOTTR

TRIAD INDUSTRIES

NOVATE!

Comes with Easy to Apply, Make Them Yourself Label Instructions
80 Pages

Save $1

$**2**⁹⁹

Reg. $3.99

Hypnotizing Screen Saver

Look at our multicolored, flashing screen saver. Isn't it fabulous? Are you getting sleepy? Sleepy? Now, take all the money in your wallet and send it to Stooples right away. And your boss's wallet, too. When you wake up, you won't remember a thing. Except that every time you're in an Office Hacks SuperStore, you'll get an uncontrollable urge to urinate in the aisle. SKU **AWAKE ON THREE** $**1,2,3**⁰⁰

Cafeteria Corner SceneriOs

Businesspeople need a business breakfast. ScenariOs provides complete nutrition and acumen for the rising analytical executive. Sugarcoated, tastes great with fruit (out of season? Chilean?), milk (good cow? mad cow?) and analysis (distracted by bear market? erection?). Official breakfast cereal of the Harvard Business School.

SKU **CHOMP**

Fallout Furniture

Make sure your business remains part of the nuclear age. Portable lead-lined furniture rolls quickly against doors and windows to shield against shock waves, radiation and mutant warriors. Underdesk compartments hold cell phone, laptop, Geiger counter and stenographer. Graceful walnut veneer lets you survive in comfort and elegance.

SKU **IKBOOM**

$1,950⁰⁰

Official Office Furniture of Pyongyang, North Korea.

Coal-Burning Computer

Don't let an energy crisis get you down. Environmentally ambiguous hardware will help produce memos even during the most persistent brownout. Much safer than nuclear computers, though there is some risk of Black Office Lung. Don't be a namby-pamby—there's work to be done! SKU **SOOT**

Application Forms for People Who Bring Their Family to Interviews

Nothing tells you that people are ready for work more than when they bring their children along while filling out applications. Reward their clear thinking with Family-Style Application Forms, one for Mom or Dad, the other for their brood who are jumping up and down on lobby chairs and asking employees if they could please have some Reese's Pieces. Queries for the young ones include: "Can you draw the face Mommy makes when Daddy doesn't put the seat down," and "Do Mommy/Daddy really vacuum or just kick things under the couch?" Place in prospective employee files, or share with other HR people during HR conventions.
SKU KIDSWRITETHEDARNDESTTHINGS

How to Order by Mail

Stamps are helpful, and envelopes, too. Use our order blank or any other paper-like substance. Ask your mother to lick the gummy part of the envelope so you won't have icky on your tongue.

$**19**^{99}
PER SET

Elevator Tragedy/Comedy Masks

Let everyone know how your weekend was before they ask. Vividly descriptive theater symbols save you from the tedium of Monday-morning questioning, let you speed to your floor in relative anonymity. Soft inner padding designed for extended wear if you're overly sulky or euphoric. Black and white or white and black. SKU **IHIDE**

STO•PLES
Office Tools for Hopeless Fools

Visit us online @ **www.stooples.com**

Call 1-800-STOOPLE

M E M O

To: All Managers
From: The Sultan of Suspension Files
RE: Respect—Just a little bit.

All:

Yes, I have a relatively high opinion of myself, and maybe that life-sized bronze statue in the lobby might have been a bit over the top, but after making my first hundred million dollars by age twenty-three, can you blame a man for liking what he sees in the mirror?And for talking about himself in the third person?

Despite all this money and a very high station in this life, I'm still a basically sensitive guy. I have feelings."If you prick me, do I not bleed?" If you call me "needle putz," do I not cry?

And that, dear Stooples managers, is what I write about today. Respect. R-E-S-P-E-C-T. I want you to find out what it means to me, and pass it on to the staff ASAP.

I feel as if everywhere I go, no matter what I do, no matter what I say, that I'm being mocked, parodied, or held up as an object of ridicule. This being America, we all have the right to express ourselves. But this being my company, I want to emphasize that, in this corporate setting of ours, there need to be some rules. I'm the boss, and I need to be respected – at least publicly. Laughter is the best medicine when no stronger prescription drugs are available, and I love a good joke as much as the next high-powered and dashingly handsome CEO; but we've gotta have some decorum and some rules. I've formulated some and expect you to pass them around right away.

Rule #1: No jokes about the list of rules. I don't want to get back any copies with hand-scrawled comments like "Bullshit!" or "Spoken like a true management goober!"

Rule #2: No offensive signs on my statue in the lobby. In fact, no signs at all on my statue in the lobby. This past week I removed one pasted over my crotch that read, "Where's the beef?" I had just walked into the office with CFO de Krook and the head of purchasing for IBM, and boy, did they ever have a laugh at my expense.

Rule #3: After careful thought, I have decided to permit bathroom graffiti as a legitimate form of expression. But I must demand that you restrict the size of letters to two inches high, and submissions must be under ten words. I highly encourage words of praise and adulation for your Dear Leader. Also, anything derogatory about my sexual prowess or physical appearance is "out" and will be scrubbed away by janitorial staff. To give an example, "Donny Steintrumper cuts a trim figure on the dance floor," would be considered acceptable graffiti, while "Donny Steintrumper needs an electron microscope to find his tiny gonads" wouldn't work because it's not very nice, it borders on the profane, and it's longer than ten words.

Oh, and one last note to our in-house graffiti artists: If you're gonna make insulting comparisons of me to someone or something, at least get it right. The name is SteinTRUMPER! Steinbrenner owns the Yankees. I, on the other hand, own your sorry asses.

Regards,

Donny

Attrition Helper

Your company has declared staff reductions will be achieved by attrition, but no one's resigning. What to do? Attrition Helper convinces older, easily intimidated employees to accept severance packages and flee the premises immediately. Includes: Sicilian-sounding screen savers that tell workers they may not be around to renew their AARP memberships, "If ya know what I mean"; Metamucil Water Coolers and digitally enhanced punk-rock-hold button music that continues playing even when you hang up the phone. Twenty% staff reductions or your money back. SKU **SEE YA**

NEW $499⁹⁹

Gotta Go
Attrition Helper
For the stubborn old bastards who just don't get the hint

Self-Burning Coffee Decanter

Why wait until someone leaves the coffeepot on all night to get that great charcoal taste? Self-immolating coffeepot begins to burn even before you pour the water. Savor that gritty morning flavor you know so well. Choose from Burnt Butter Rum, Acidic Amaretto Delight, Charred Chocolate Raspberry, Hellacious Hawaiian Surprise and our very special Scorched Earth Morning Blend. SKU **JUST BLACK, PLEASE**

$8⁹⁹

Save $2
Reg. $10.99

Packing Box Peanuts

Never put your hand into a Stooples cardboard box filled with plastic peanuts where you can't immediately see the product. Your product may be under there somewhere, or it may be Randy's pet ferret that escaped last week. Please use oven mitts, and if you are bitten, call Randy immediately for a $5.00 reward. Or return ferret to nearest OfficeHacks location and release in aisle 3.

STOOPLES
Office Tools for Hopeless Fools

 Visit us online @ **www.stooples.com**

 **Call 1-800-STOOPLE**

Holographic Paper Cube

Looks like a paper cube, but really a 3-D image from outer space. When you really want a paper cube on your desk but don't have room. Caution: Use only 3" x 3" holographic paper. Colors: Crystal, Clear, Nude-a-Rama.

SKU **WITHOUT SPACESHIP**

$2⁰⁰

SKU **WITH SPACESHIP**
$14,000,000,002⁰⁰

Reg. $51.99

Big Pants

Your experience in the corporate world has people looking to you for answers. How to avoid this unwanted responsibility? Big Pants can destroy your credibility within seconds. Simply remove jacket and show pants. When people see that your belt is higher than your belly button, your advice-giving days are over at last! Pants large enough to hold lunch, suitcase and minor league baseball team. Size 78 only. Also available: the necktie that goes down to your kneecap. SKU **CHMUCK**

NOW ONLY $49⁹⁹

Hyper-Text Prozac

When electronic documents link too quickly, your computer may hyperventilate, break into tears or eat an entire box of Famous Amos cookies. Hyper-Text Prozac will help your computer relax, take you to mostly pleasant Web sites. Nonaddictive (we think) Prozac will help your computer perform smoother clicks for an even-tempered ride through the bowels of the World Wide Web. Coming soon: Virtual Reality Valium.

SKU **SIMMER DOWN**

$15

WITH YOUR HMO PRESCRIPTION CARD

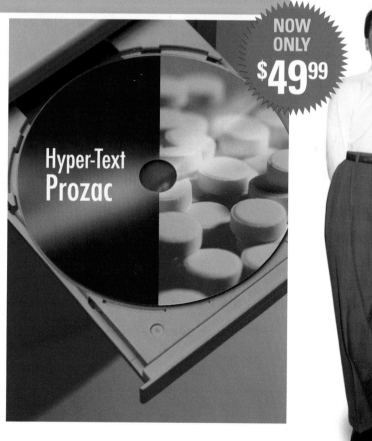

Hyper-Text Prozac

Black Hole Out-Box

Galactic phenomenon harnessed for office efficiency. Two-tier desk tray featuring compressed dwarf star out-box whisks nagging memos, unintelligible reports and useless correspondence to alternate universe. Sturdy in-box resists gravitational pull. Attractive guard rail keeps fingers from destabilizing. Pitch-black only. SKU **FAR OUT**

NEW
$88⁹⁹

OUT

IN

Messenger Roach Kit

Why give cockroaches a free ride? Specialty Roach Kit puts them to work like everyone else. Includes: "Messenger Roach" shell label, miniature elevator activator, Tungsten roach clip to help drag mail through streets and very tiny Nikes to give them a half a chance of crossing the street. SKU **SQUISH**

Save $1

$10⁹⁵

Reg. $11.95

While Supplies Last!

Who are we kidding? We know we can't get rid of these. They'll be around forever!

MESSENGER ROACH

Electromagnetic Time Stretcher

The boss wants that report out by five, but why should he drive you crazy? Secretarial time stretcher slips under desk, creates small electromagnetic field to slow clocks and watches. Gives you that extra hour without hassle from management. Also allows long lunch hours and extended trips to mall. Moderately powered device won't interfere with nearby radar installations or low-flying aircraft. SKU **RELAX**

For An Unlimited Time Only
$48⁹⁹

Chuckles The Meeting Clown

Hate nerve-wracking silences during meetings? Chuckles the Meeting Clown prances, pratfalls and tumblesaults across your conference-room table. Breaks tension, builds morale, distracts from the fact that no one knows what they're talking about. Annual meeting? No problem! Twenty-six clowns pour out of a Hummer! Red honkey nose not included. SKU **CLOWNZ**

$65⁰⁰ per hour

Wal-Mart Annual Meetings Special Discount

$6⁵⁰ PER HOUR

Office Hacks Crank Calls

Please Note: *Telemarketers who call you from OfficeHacks are malicious pranksters who should be hung up on immediately. However, please feel free to blow air horns into the receiver before you do. Characterizations of the caller's lineage are also appreciated and may result in a $10 Stooples Gift Certificate (We said, "may result." Don't get your hopes up, Shorty.).*

Reliable Products
Stooples products are 100% sound! If our products don't make a sound, drop them on the floor a few times, then clean ears thoroughly.

To: Mr. William B. Applebaum
Managing Editor
The New York Times
September 23, 2003

Dear Sir:

I'm appalled by the abysmal quality of journalism conducted by your newspaper yesterday. I refer to the article you carried on the front of your business section, "Battle for Office-Supply Dollars Heats Up: Upstart Stooples Wrests Market Share from Titan OfficeHacks." I don't know where to begin in pointing out the inaccuracies introduced by your journalist—Mr. Jayson Blair—in an altogether error-ridden piece of garbage.

Specifically:

Mr. Blair claims to have spoken with me on several occasions, "from the Louisiana gay brothel 'King of Queens.'" Problem: I've never been there.

At one point in the story, Mr. Blair describes his visit to "Malaysian factory Lakmeup Andeye—a sweatshop devoted to 24/7 production by children between five and ten years old of office supplies for OfficeHacks." He's quite precise in the details of the building, down to the "dried blood between the floor tiles that attest to the inhumane conditions that prevail at this OfficeHacks production unit" and "the locks on the bathroom doors that prevent employees from taking a bathroom break." Problem: We have a factory in the part of Malaysia that he describes, but it's brand-new and is monitored round-the-clock by United Nations observers and Jimmy Carter. It's almost as if Mr. Blair wasn't even there.

Last, I particularly take issue with the following passage, allegedly quoting my esteemed rival, Stooples CEO Donny Steintrumper, who I know would never say the nasty things attributed to him. "I have great respect for 'Teeny' Davis. He's a wonderful guy, despite his latex fetish and the fact that he wears ladies' panties. He's a pillar of the community. In fact, at 265 pounds, he's about three pillars and half the Colosseum."

Sir, I demand an immediate retraction and an apology for these errors.

Sincerely,
Jamison "Teeny" Davis
CEO OfficeHacks Inc.

E X C H A N G E

To: Mr. William B. Applebaum
Managing Editor
The New York Times
September 24, 2003

Dear Willy:

I cannot attest to some of the errors alleged by Tiny in his letter to the editor yesterday because I have only visited OfficeHacks sweatshops in China and Vietnam, myself. But he's 100 percent correct on one count: While I did speak to your reporter, Mr. Jayson Blair, his quote was somewhat wrong and out-of-context. I would never accuse Tiny of wearing women's panties. In fact, what I said was, "He's a wonderful guy, despite the fact that he wears a lady's THONG."

Regards,

Donny Steintrumper
CEO and Chairman
Stooples

To: Mr. William B. Applebaum
Managing Editor
The New York Times
September 25, 2003

Dear Mr. Applebaum:

I take umbrage at Mr. Steintrumper's comments. I most certainly do not wear a lady's thong. Perhaps Mr. Steintrumper caught me in the locker room right after a game of squash at the club. As is standard practice, the loser receives a wedgie. I'm not much of a squash player.

Jamison "Teeny" Davis

Mr. Jayson Blair
Copy Boy
Lewiston Ledger
3 Main Street
Lewiston, ME 00300

Dear Jayson:

Sorry to hear your book isn't selling. But, boy, you sure can dream up some great "stories." They were worth every penny. Enclosed is the check for $25,000 I promised. Buy some coke or amphetamines. There's more money coming from an untraceable offshore account where this came from. Above all, keep those OfficeHacks attacks coming!

Best,
Donny

Special
$74⁹⁹

Designed for our

URBAN OFFICE
COLLECTION

Crappy Companies Need Love, Too.   October 2005

BusinessWeak

50 Slowest-Growing Hedge Funds

25 CEOs WHO HUNG THEMSELVES IN THE BATHROOM

$39.99
One-Year Subscription
$29.99
Two-Year Subscription

BusinessWeak Magazine

Crappy companies need love, too. *Business-Weak* focuses on the stories behind the losers, why they stink and how you can avoid them at all costs. Special issues include "100 Technologies You'll Never Miss," "50 Slowest-Growing Hedge Funds" and "25 CEOs Who Hung Themselves in the Bathroom." A must-read, especially if you're in prison and have a lot of time on your hands. SKU **LOOZER**

Over Easy

Don't let dead-to-the-world bums block your way to the office. Streamlined, fold-up ladder lets you climb over street people with relative ease. Sturdy construction allows you to keep your distance, resists fleas, lice and other unwanted hitchhikers. Leather-grip handle allows carry-along convenience. SKU **ALLEY-OOP**

BunkDesks

Teamwork breeds success. Innovative bunkdesks create close working relationships between employees while saving office space. Two-tier system puts one worker on the shoulders of another, fostering cooperation and balanced objectives. Not recommended for companies with a strong union presence. SKU **TOTEM**

SpaceSaver Price
$299⁹⁹

STOOPLES
Office Tools for Hopeless Fools

Visit us online @ **www.stooples.com**

Call **1-800-STOOPLE**

Stall-to-Stall Intercom

Don't let long trips to the bathroom disturb your presentation. Electronic sound enhancer ensures your words and expressive sounds carry directly to all meeting participants, wherever you are. Automatic five-second shutoff system guarantees discretion when you need it most. Not recommended after three-bean lunches.

SKU **FOLLOW**

Save $5
$129⁹⁹

Reg. $134.99

Board of Directors Escort Serv~~ice~~

Forget about minority s~~...~~
screwing up your well-~~...~~
bonuses for you and o~~...~~
vote ahead of time wi~~...~~
Service. Our team of ~~...~~
least a semifinalist in ~~...~~
pageant—come in all ~~...~~
ensure every one of ~~...~~
dreams. Flexible, plia~~...~~
on the Board of Dire~~...~~
sure your directors ~~...~~

$1,599 Team
$2,199 Team

That man was not wearing pants during photo shoot.

Meeting Mellower

Tough negotiations? Meeting Mellower can help. Desktop freshener emits special-blend aromatic incense to turn deadlocked parties into party guys. Discourages bickering, encourages camaraderie, blood-brother rituals and Jell-O shots. Voice-sensitive, triggers twice a minute during serious discussions, six times upon onset of caterwauling and teeth-gnashing. SKU **BCOOL**

ONLY
$11⁹⁹

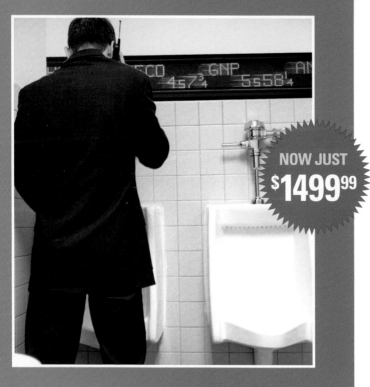

The Wall Street Urinal

Porcelain wall urinal offers real-time stock prices, keeps brokers informed even when "duty calls." Handle can be manipulated for NYSE, Amex and over-the-counter readings; built-in microphone lets you buy and sell as you flush. Optional deodorizer tablet features miniature video screen, offers market prognosticators in the news. Also available: CNBCeat. SKU **WSURN**

NOW JUST
$1499⁹⁹

Helps you obscure even the most basic details during cross-examination

120 Minutes
2 DVDs

Dead Horse

Some people won't let go of an idea. Practical gift gives them something to beat. Therapeutic ex-equus allows venting of frustration without snorting or kicking, provides the perfect release for the obstinate or the oversensitive. Carts away easily when it's time to quit horsin' around. Specify: Arabian Gray, Appaloosa Gray, Gray Area. SKU **GLUE**

Save $50
$259⁹⁹
Reg. $309.99

Takes a real good beating!

Testimony Helper

Confused about what your multitrillion dollar company really does day-to-day? Unsure of what the definition of "is" is? Testimony Helper helps you obscure even the most basic details. Also provides helpful guide to pouty-lip, big, sad-eyed expressions during cross-examination. PDA version helps you when you need it most—on the stand! SKU **DUH!**

ONLY
$49⁵⁹
WE SWEAR!

Visit us online @ **www.stooples.com**

Call 1-800-STOOPLE

Glue Schtick

Break up your presentation and your audience with clear, nontoxic Glue Schtick. Adheres charts, graphs, flip charts to your clothes, forehead, your boss's forehead or even your backside without wrinkling or tearing them. Non-toxic, odorless formula is the perfect distraction for presentations that carry the intellectual weight of gerbils. Also available: Slippery Glue Schtick, when unabashed slapstick is needed to camouflage complete financial ruin. SKU **TACKY**

ONLY 99¢ each

Browbeater

Tap human resources even when you're not there. Leather headband carries two synchronized drumsticks, attaches to forehead for day-long electronic brow-beating. Soft plastic tips won't cause concussions or cerebral hemorrhaging, creates pleasant percussive backbeat for total office enjoyment. Three models: Sousa, Ringo, San Andreas Fault. SKU **BEAT**

ONLY $25.99

Hara-Kiri Spindles

Falling short of quota is a serious offense. Take the honorable way out by throwing yourself on our chrome-plated desk spindle. Razor-sharp spire thrusts cleanly, prevents messy endings and spills. Rubber safety cap guards against accidental spearing, keeps tip rust-free for when you need it most. SKU **SAMURAI**

$5.99 EACH

Bankers' Solvency Globe

Bankers: Keep track of your international loans the easy way. Nations disappear from the face of the earth upon default, reappear after restructuring payments. Colorful contemporary features include mountains, oceans, deserts and welchers. Gold-lustre base dissolves upon collapse of world banking system. SKU **LOANZ**

NEW Low Price $38.99

Executive Tatami

No empty seats? Competition for rush-hour comfort is fierce, but Japanese Executive Tatami gives you a seat even if you don't arrive before the rising sun. Basket-weave, all-rattan floor mat fits easily in the aisle or by the door, provides enough room for meditative slumbering or digestion of morning sushi. Official tatami of the Tokyo Transit Authority. SKU **AHSO**

ONLY
$49⁹⁹

Shareholder Muzzle

Dissident stockholders can turn an annual meeting into a dogfight. Shareholder muzzle keeps things from getting out of hand. Full-length muzzle fits over chin and snout, quiets everyone down during PowerPoint presentations. Keeps Q&A sessions short and sweet. One size fits all. SKU **SIT**

Save $1
$12⁹⁹
Reg. $13..99

Holds Pink Slips, Kleenex, Resume Pointers, Headhunter Contacts, Junk, Antidepressants, Cyanide and Much, Much More!

"Buy it while it still can be expensed"

Back Me in a Corner
CADDY

NEW
Low Price
$14⁹⁹

Back Me in a Corner Caddy

Behind on quota? Behind on market share? Just a big behind your company's getting rid of? This is the organizer for you! Holds pink slips, Kleenex, résumé pointers, headhunter logo junk, Prozac, cyanide, more. Buy it while it can still be expensed! SKU **WHACKED**

Save your ass and cover hers with plastic peel-on ColorForms for Porn.

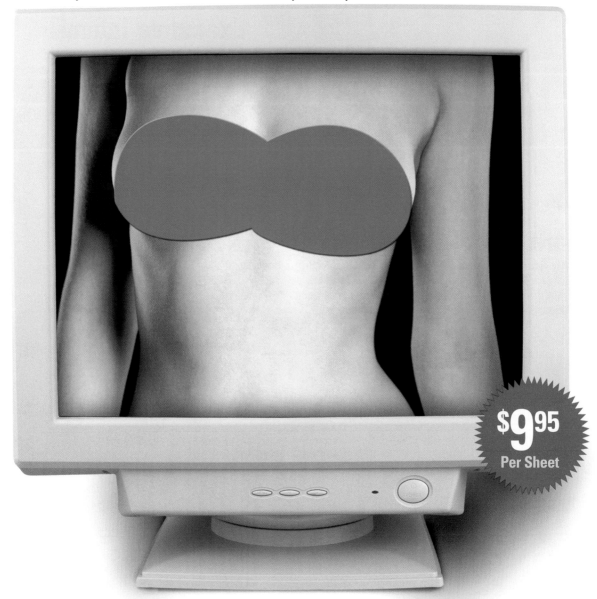

$9⁹⁵
Per Sheet

Porn at Work "ColorForms"

At most companies, viewing porn at work is a cause for dismissal. Save your ass and cover hers with plastic peel-on ColorForms for Porn. When the boss is down the hall, peel-on blue plastic dresses, red plastic bras, green plastic chastity belts—before you know it, your site will look like CNN.com! Braille ColorForms available for blind and touchy-feely employees. SKU **COVER-UP**

M E M O

To: All Staff at Headquarters
From: The Dictator of Desk Mats
Re: Oink Oink

Boys and gals:

Don't I give you jobs and barely enough to live on? Don't I supply you with a desk, chair, and computer? Don't I try to allow a fairly decent work environment by letting you put those ficus plants and pics of your brats and spouses in your cubicles?

If so, why the hell would some greedy, gluttonous, stupid pig snag the half-sandwich I left in the second-floor refrigerator yesterday? This wasn't just any sandwich, mind you. It was a roast beef and Boursin sandwich on dill focaccia, with the fat shaved from the flanks and the Boursin creamy and rich from France, not the goopy American glop. I carried this sandwich back from Formaggio's in Cambridge earlier this week, reverently consuming the first half on the plane back from Boston and carefully folding and tucking the wax paper around the second half to avoid leakage and to keep the bread from getting soggy or stale. I sat at my desk all morning today, stomach grumbling, DREAMING of that sandwich. I sat through a meeting with what had to be the most boring accountants at this company (note to CFO de Krook: Can't you get some female accountants who like to flirt and flash some leg?). Anyway, I walk to the fridge, bend over, licking my chops, and discover—to my horror—my Formaggio sandwich is gone. You could have taken that block of furry cheese or the low-fat yogurt the fat-assed purchasing-department secretary parks in there so no one thinks she snarfs four Snickers bars a day from her top-left desk drawer. Or you could have had that tuna-fish salad in the Tupperware or that takeout green-brown Indian stuff that looks like baby diarrhea. But, oh no! *My* sandwich. You bastards.

I fully intend to do a walk-through of premises over the next hour, sniffing everyone's breath. Even with clever masking agents, I know that distinctive garlicky, cheesy smell of Formaggio's Boursin. So don't bother with the Binaca. If I smell that little slice of garlic heaven on your breath, your focaccia is going to be out the door in ten minutes.

I can't begin to tell you the fantasies of pain I want to inflict on the perpetrator(s) of this foul act. I expect the thief to own up and make a reimbursement offer. In the meantime, sandwich robbers beware: Effective immediately, I've done the following:

1) Purchased a new refrigerator for the executive section of the third floor.

2) Hired a security guard named Otis, who played defensive tackle with the Oakland Raiders practice squad until he blew out his knee, to guard said refrigerator.

3) Installed a security gate and turnstile with fingerprint and retina-scanning technology needed to gain access to the area.

4) Had our IT department rig several infrared-capable cameras hooked to digital-video recorders running on 24/7 loops to monitor the floor.

I'm assured these measures will work, but if they don't, I'm also considering releasing guard dogs and poisonous spiders and embedding high-voltage electric cables in the floor and refrigerator door to prevent thievery. I'm sorry, people, such security measures are costly and inconvenient to us all. But you drove me to it. I haven't made it to where I am without learning a few things. And one of them is you don't let a man get away with stealing half of your Formaggio sandwich.

I hate you all,

Donny

VP in the Bubble

Just because he's a man of the people doesn't mean he should catch your cold. Center for Disease Control–approved antiseptic air bubble allows executives to perform key management duties in comfortable, sanitized environment, free from underling bacteria. Protects from Secretarial SARS, Maintenance Man Malaria and New Guy Pneumonia. Colors: Clear, Seethrough, Invisible. SKU **GESUNDHEIT**

NOW ONLY $244.99

Logo Wear

Once a company man, always a company man. Velvet boxer shorts are hand stitched with the corporate logos from your career, letting you relive your successes wherever you may go. Stretch waistband adjusts as you begin to enjoy the good life. For those who really don't want to bother with a résumé. SKU **LOGO**

FREE SKID-MARK PATCH KIT WHEN YOU BUY FIVE OR MORE.

GREAT PRICE $4.99

  Visit us online @ **www.stooples.com**    Call 1-800-STOOPLE

STOoPLES Office Tools for Hopeless Fools

Bankruptcy Trampoline

Destitute investors and creditors can jump out the window to ground-floor fun. Heavy elastic trampoline acts as safety net for the financially fallen, allows swan dives and back flips from as high as the tenth floor. Can hold an entire board of directors for team competition. A great way to bounce back from adversity!

SKU **BOING!**

BANKRUPTCY TRAMPOLINE

Performance Review Banjo

Performance Review

There's nothing like a banjo to put fun into every situation, even a performance review. Strum your way to such favorites as "We Love You, Joe, but Your Assistant's Gotta Go" and "Barbara, Barbara, We Won't Harbor, a Grudge Because Sales Are Down" and "Please, Please, Evelyn, Stop Using the American Express Card or We'll Fire Yooooooou." Six string-them-along banjo comes complete with turner-outer, pic-on-you and hay-filled performance review bow tie and matching hat. SKU **HAYSEED**

Porcupine Toilet-
Seat Covers

Use your company bat[hroom] dawdling and smoking there's work to be don[e] from taking a faux pott[y] Porcupine Toilet-Seat but when they don't, t[he] 1,265 genuine porcupi[ne] your employees up a[nd] penetrate cloth and e[asily] painfully until your sl[ackers] Easy replacement or[der] quills that require no[thing] especially to avoid [spills and] other liquids. SKU **OU[...]**

Ivana girl you need to get this.

 Visit us online @ **www.stooples.com**

 **Call 1-800-STOOPLE**

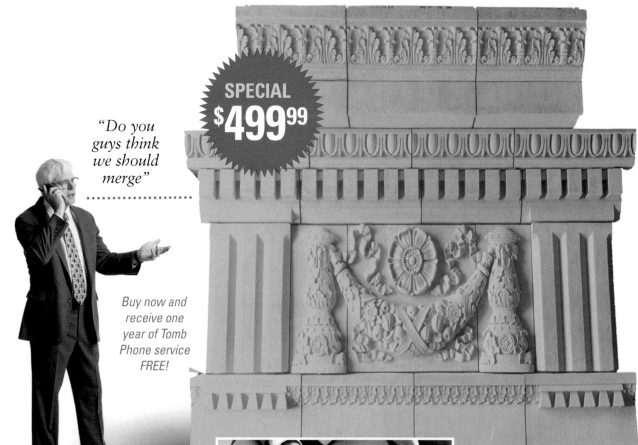

"Do you guys think we should merge"

SPECIAL $499⁹⁹

Buy now and receive one year of Tomb Phone service FREE!

NEW $67⁹⁹

Conference Tomb

Don't let years of experience go to waste. Conference Tomb holds 30 departed chairmen and directors; lets them continue to play an active role in the company. Comes with tomb-to-boardroom phone linkage for input from the great beyond. Roomy interior seats five when direct confrontation is required. SKU **RIP**

Overshadow Shoes

Don't let taller executives take all the glory. Business platform shoes help you rise to any occasion. Elongated heels and soles add as much as 18 inches to your presence, ensure you won't be overshadowed by some Kareem Abdul Credit-Snatcher. SKU **TOWR**

 STOOPLES
Office Tools for Hopeless Fools

Visit us online @ **www.stooples.com**

 Call **1-800-STOOPLE**

Paper-Cut Leeches

Paper cuts are no fun. After you bleed all over your letters and envelopes, let our paper cut leeches attach themselves to your wound for quick and efficient binding action. Imported from the quaint and picturesque jungles of Southern Zambia, our malaria-free leeches match any corporate or casual business attire, as long as it's black or gray. Use of medicinal leeches shows management that you'll go to any length to achieve world-class commitment and that you're also kind of nuts.

SKU **LEECHARIFIC!**

$10 a Handful

Office Massacre Defense System

worth every penny at

$189⁹⁹

Uh-oh, Timmy was really upset he was passed over for a promotion again. Will Timmy come back with a tommy gun? You never know, so protect yourself with Office Massacre Defense System (OMDS). At the first sound of Uzi fire, OMDS will automatically open your window and release a sturdy thirty-foot rope ladder, providing an instant escape route. Simultaneously, a six-foot replica of your handsome self will appear in a conference room down the hall from your office, providing additional time to scoot away. Once you're safe, you can call the police and feel good that you've saved the occasional junior executive who was missed by the first spray of gunfire. A must for every executive who employs humans and other unpredictable creatures. SKU **SCAMPER**

WARNING!
The Perimeter Has Been Breached!

CANCEL   PROCEED

THIS MESSAGE HAS BEEN BROUGHT TO YOU BY OFFICE MASSACRE DEFENSE SYSTEM

STOoPLES
Office Tools for Hopeless Fools

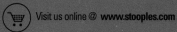
Visit us online @ **www.stooples.com**

Call **1-800-STOOPLE**

97

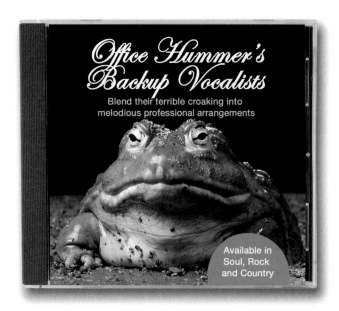

Office Hummer's
Backup Vocalists

Blend their terrible croaking into
melodious professional arrangements

Available in
Soul, Rock
and Country

Office Hummer's Backup Vocalists

If the gal in the next cubicle is an intractable hummer, don't jeopardize your career by launching staplers and tape dispensers. Office Hummer's Backup Vocalists CD lets you blend her terrible croaking into melodious professional arrangements the entire office will enjoy. Soul, rock, country—the harmonies will keep you sane and your office mate from grievous head wounds. Also available: Motown Muttering, R&B Burper, Talk-to-Myself Techno, Glam Rock Gagging, Zydeco Zippering and Obsessive Sniffling Salsa.
SKU **WOOWOO**

NEW
Alto Low Price
$**19**⁹⁵

Pocket Shredder

Inconspicuous shredder lets you destroy sensitive documents even when lawyers are present. Clip-on device attaches inside trouser pocket, empties down pant leg into sock. Insulated motor cuts down on noise, keeps hip gyrations to a minimum. SKU **SNEAKY**

$**29**⁹⁹

Stooples and Outsourcing

Stooples is proud to offer jobs to needy, Third World, uneducated boobs who speak quasi-English. Our never-ending quest to save you money means we're laying off good old American staff with their big salaries and fat benefits like crazy and outsourcing their jobs to Bangalore, Mumbai, and Bangladesh. And you know what? Our customers can't tell the difference. Look at this excerpt of an actual call to our client call center in the disputed Jammu-Kashmir border region between Pakistan and India:

Stooples Rep (SR): Good morning to you, sir. How are you this fine day? And how might I be of service to you?

Customer: I'm a woman.

SR: Ah, right. Of course you are. A bit hard to tell from here, but I shall take your esteemed word for it. Now, how can this humble personage of this great American company help you? Are you seeking something for purchase or perhaps a very simple and easy exchange of somewhat faulty goods?

Customer: I'm sorry. I can't understand a word you're saying. Could you please speak more clearly?

SR: It must be the satellite. We're very high up in the mountains, you know. Or, perhaps it's the automatic gunfire and mortar shells. You know, it gets quite loud at around eleven a.m. in the morning. That is, madam, of course when the border guards start lobbing grenades at our humble call center.

Customer: No. It's your accent. Are you speaking English? Where are you, Omaha?

SR: No, actually, my dear lady, you have reached a simple call center operator in the world's second-most-populous nation –

Customer: China? Are you speaking Chinese?

SR: No, I'm quite pleased to tell you that you are not far off geographically, but we are in SOUTH Asia, while China is somewhat farther north. You have reached—.

Customer (more excited): I know. I know. Don't tell me. Indonesia. You're in Indonesia.

SR (chuckling): Madam, you are quite clever, but again, I would be prevaricating if I told your esteemed being that you were correct. I'm in India. Jammu-Kashmir, to be precise.

Customer Wait. That's part of Pakistan.

SR (angered): Madam, you have employed faulty reasoning. This area belongs to India.

Customer (more insistent): Listen, I saw a documentary on PBS. It's Pakistani.

SR (very angry): Madam, by all that is right and proper in this fine world, I beg Shiva to forgive me for calling you a stupid piece of cow dung. It is Indian.

Customer (yelling): How DARE you. It's Pakistani.

SR (yelling back): INDIAN!

 Visit us online @ **www.stooples.com**

 Call 1-800-STOOPLE

Middle-Finger Conference Call Detector

Who hasn't participated in an audio conference call and believed some of the participants were being less than respectful? Know what's happening on the other end with our motion-sensitive Middle-Finger Conference Call Detector. When a fellow employee flips the bird to his or her telephone, you'll know immediately! Also picks up eye-rolling, extra-long tongue extensions, even mooning! You'll know the instant they don't respect you. A must for those who demand information they can do nothing about. SKU **BIRD**

$34.99

How to File Your Corporate Taxes Like a Porn Star

"Ooooh, Baby! Give
Amortize me, slathe
Doing your taxes ha
rewarding. And the
Your Corporate Taxe
nearly 99% audit-pr
most IRS inspectors
or too turned on by
the numbers. Our gu
tax forms like a Jen
scene in no time fla
customers. How do
and coming back fc
latest loopholes.

SKU **1069-H**

On the hot seat! Charcoal Butt!

Diagonal Wire Files for when you can't sort in a straight line

D.U.I. File Sorter

3 Qty.

Only $16.99

D.U.I File Sorter

Can't sort in a straight line? Diagonal wire file perfect after three-martini lunches, tokes behind the copier, over-sniffing glue sticks. Easy viewing and access even if you can't find your ass with both hands. Not LAPD-approved.

SKU **CRAZY, MAN!**

FREE Flask with every purchase!

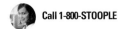

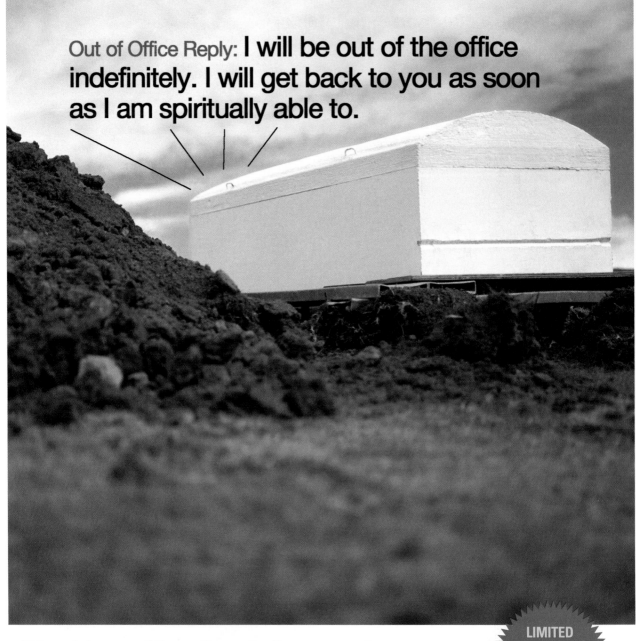

Out of Office Reply: I will be out of the office indefinitely. I will get back to you as soon as I am spiritually able to.

Blackbury After-Death Communicator

Just because you're deceased doesn't mean you shouldn't answer your e-mails. Blackbury device slips neatly into casket, attaches to cold, dead fingers before the lid is closed. Atomic cell powers device for thousands of years, can be recharged if terrible virus causes the dead to rise and kill but they still wish to communicate with each other. Water-resistant, handsome leather case will match future zombie skin pallor. SKU **WTF**

 STOOPLES Office Tools for Hopeless Fools

 Visit us online @ **www.stooples.com**

 Call 1-800-STOOPLE

Stick-it Discipline Notes

Bright, attention-getting notes stick to the back or front of incompetent subordinates. Use preprinted memoranda—"R&D Doofus," "Forgot to Cancel Dividend," "Was Honest to the Media," "Laid Off Boss's Mother"—or write your own! Gummy adhesive leaves nonremovable marks on clothing for further disciplinary effect. Not to be used on anyone who will either sue or think it's a compliment. SKU **DORK**

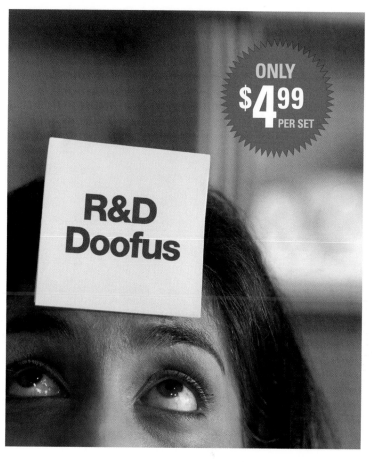

ONLY
$**4**.99
PER SET

R&D
Doofus

Short Seller

Diminutive broker not only borrows stocks expected to fall, but can work little hands behind file cabinet for coins, subway tokens and other forms of lost currency. A true daredevil, whether you wish him to purchase bonds on margin or roll around under the conference room table in case someone drops a quarter. Also able to get in and out of New York Stock Exchange quickly by running between other brokers' legs. Fully understands the ins and outs of high finance, even if he has to stand on a stool to buy the *Wall Street Journal*. SKU **ELF**

NEW!

$**99** per trade *or* 25% of currency found

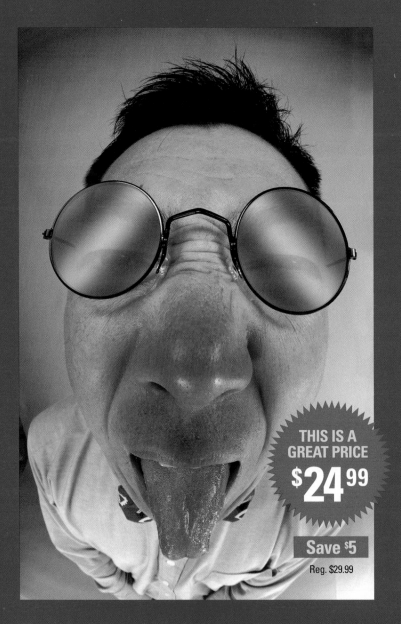

THIS IS A GREAT PRICE

$24⁹⁹

Save $5

Reg. $29.99

Subliminal Advertising Deflector Glasses

Protect yourself from the orgy in the fried clams or the shadowy text that implores you to vote yet again for Pat Buchanan. Mirrored glasses deflect sneaky ad messages that compel you to do things you wouldn't normally do, like floss. Stylish yet subtle, deflector glasses will help keep you safe from commands like **YOU, BUY THREE MORE PRODUCTS IN THIS BOOK, NOW! YES, YOU**. Or better yet, buy it after you finish reading this catalog. SKU **ORGY?**

Vegan Helper

Your new employee doesn't eat meat, fish, eggs, milk or even chicken and the lunch meeting runs until 2:30. Make sure the salad-crazed Vegan doesn't collapse mid-meeting with delicious and impossible-to-detect Sneaky Food Products from Vegan Helper. Choose from Meat Mints, Poultry Pencil Tops, mouthwash laced with squid and more. And for carb-starved employees: Our new Stealth Bagel. Meeting Malnutrition No More! SKU **YUMM, SQUID**

$5⁹⁹

100 Tablets

Stooples T-Shirt

Stooples fashionable T-shirts, only $9.99, plus sales tax, shipping, FedEx man eats his lunch in a truck tax, "Where the hell did the receptionist put this?" finders fee, "Ow, shit, I cut myself on the 'effing' scissors" tax, Band-Aid tax, clean the blood off the scissors tax, communicable disease alert tax, quarantine the whole goddamned office tax and "Oh, God, when it will it all end," overreacting surcharge. Specify S, M, S&M, M&M, Eminem, XL, XXL, Salad Bar Candidate.

Black

Zorro File

Swashbuckling Z file used only once by Antonio Banderas during major motion picture (scene where Zorro meets evil land owners at Zorro Conference Center). A hit with zealous South American temptresses and xenophobic mistresses (don't tell them how to spell it). Also impress Zambian foreign ministers, zookeepers and people named Zeke. Comes in black, cobalt and really, really dark brown. SKU **$SLASH**

$14.99

7 A.M. Morning Marker

Two hours early and no one there to see you? Get full credit from bosses, coworkers, with automatic third-party e-mail alert system. Example e-mail: "Can you believe Ashtar Bolivius was at his desk at 6:58 a.m.?" Jim. Or "Wow, what was Suzie Franco working on at 7:03 this morning?" Jim. No one in your company named Jim? No problem! Easy-to-change first letter allows you to substitute Him or Bim or Lim! SKU **JIM ZIM**

INBOX: E-mail 16 of 25   previous e-mail   next e-mail

From: jasmith@toreocorp.com   [Add to Address Book] [View Source]
To: semcclellan@toreocorp.com
Subject: This guy is amazing
Date: December 20, 2004

Can you believe Ashtar Bolivius was at his desk at 6:58 a.m.?

Jim

Toreo Corporation
116 Samuel Drive
Union, NJ 07083
(908) 555-5555

Velcro Tie

If you hate tie pins but can't seem to make your tie stay still during presentations, Velcro Tie is for you. Velcro strips adhere to shirt or zipper, depending on sartorial preference. Wind gusts? Velcro Tie will cling to pocket protector. A must for people who feel tie clips are way too ostentatious or complicated. SKU **WHOOSH**

$1.99 Each

Enron Accounting Journal

Who needs spreadsheets when you can conduct business the Enron way? Bogus accounting journal helps you inflate the numbers by recording assets, sales, credits, while ignoring the other stuff. Low-quality paper promotes smudging. Intersecting columns let you obscure real or imagined profits, prevents thorough rechecking by Treasury agents, unless they're smart.

SKU **ENRUNAROUND**

ONLY
$10⁹⁹

Origami Printout Sheets

$49⁹⁹

Now you can store printouts and decorate your office simultaneously. Specially processed computer sheets hold together under high-speed printout conditions, then fold neatly into ducks, pandas and swallows. Eliminate drab binders forever. SKU **HOWNICE**

Snack Truck Mold Remover

Snack Trucks are great for getting out of the office, but some of the food they serve is older than your mother. Snack Truck Mold Remover gets the unwanted growth off your food before you ingest it. Keeps your mouth away from egg salad eczema, cup o' soup cholera and the 27 lethal forms of bagel bacteria. Spray once, twice and the odds of food poisoning are reduced 63%. Not effective in removing unwanted growths from your mother.

SKU **HAIRYHOTDOG?**

NEW
Low Price
$20⁹⁹

 STOOPLES
Office Tools for Hopeless Fools

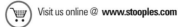 Visit us online @ **www.stooples.com**

 Call **1-800-STOOPLE**

No-Touch Corporate Massage

Your aching back versus an egregious lawsuit. Now you don't have to make a choice. No-Touch Corporate Massage teaches assistants, underlings and other potential plaintiffs how to get rid of your knots without ever touching your body! Quick hand motions produce swift wind currents over shoulders, back, neck—even toes! You'll feel better in minutes, or at least you'll enjoy the attention. Caution: Do not use No-Touch Corporate Massage in offices where there are video cameras, witnesses or nosy birds at the window. Also available: No-Touch Corporate Handshake and Air-Kissing for CEOs. SKU **JNOSYBIRDSSTINK**

$12⁹⁵ Per Handbook

Catalogs and Duplicates
We are saddened by the incredible amount of waste involved in sending duplicate copies to the same person. If you are the same person, please let us know. If you a different person, please let us know and we'll tell you if we like the change, or whether you had more "character" before you fixed your teeth.

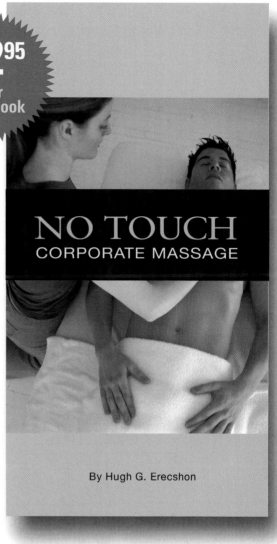

NO TOUCH
CORPORATE MASSAGE

By Hugh G. Erecshon

Say good-bye to traffic jams!

NEW Low Price $159⁹⁹

Gossamer Commuter Wings

Tired of sitting on Route 257 in your Toyota listening to happy DJs say they'll never date a lesbian unless she brings her friend? Avoid the horrors of rush-hour snarls with Blessed Gossamer Wings. Made of pure unalloyed essence of dove, these sturdy wings won't crack, split or melt, even if you fly too close to the sun. Portable landing perch provides window-to-window ease. SKU **FLAP**

Downsizing LSD (Layoff Soother & Depressant)

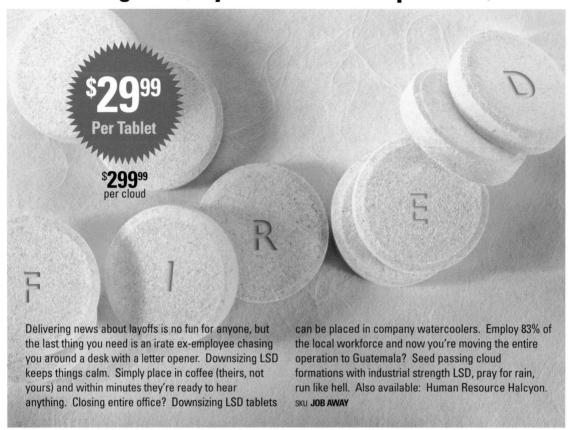

$29⁹⁹ Per Tablet

$299⁹⁹ per cloud

Delivering news about layoffs is no fun for anyone, but the last thing you need is an irate ex-employee chasing you around a desk with a letter opener. Downsizing LSD keeps things calm. Simply place in coffee (theirs, not yours) and within minutes they're ready to hear anything. Closing entire office? Downsizing LSD tablets can be placed in company watercoolers. Employ 83% of the local workforce and now you're moving the entire operation to Guatemala? Seed passing cloud formations with industrial strength LSD, pray for rain, run like hell. Also available: Human Resource Halcyon. SKU **JOB AWAY**

Best for short-term, long-distance projects

NEW!! $10⁹⁹

Hunch & Leap

Bad file! Wire file arches when you come near, leaps at you with razor-coated legs. Best for short-term, long-distance projects. SKU **GRRR**

Back Orders
We do not like back orders. If a product is unavailable, that means Bill the Buyer has gone off his Twelve-Step Program. You will be notified when the product is available once more, perhaps by Bill's replacement, who hopefully isn't a heroin addict.

  Visit us online @ **www.stooples.com**  Call 1-800-STOOPLE

Business Blinders

Leather headgear obstructs employee peripheral vision, inspires greater on-the-job concentration. Genuine cowhide straps fit snugly around head to prevent unauthorized peeking. Matching harness helps reign in those who chomp at the bit. Three models: Buckpasser, Secretariat and Man-o-Office.

SKU **NAY**

NEW Low Price $29⁹⁹

MEMO

To: All Staff
From: The Mullah of Manila Folders
RE: "Bring-Your-Pet-to-Work Day"

All:

Though it didn't look possible until just a few days ago, I wanted to invite you to our second annual "Stooples Bring-Your-Pet-to-Work Day." Organized by our very own attack dog, CFO Julius de Krook, who was unexpectedly released early for good behavior from Rahway State Prison after serving a six-month sentence for cruelty to animals, this event promises something for everyone.

For the family-oriented, take this as an opportunity to get your pooch or kitty shampooed, coiffed, and beribboned, because I'm offering prizes of $100, $50, and $25 for the first-, second-, and third-place winners of our "Who's the Pwettiest?" beauty contest. Last year's winner, a Pekingese named "Princess Shirley of Schenectady" will receive an automatic bye from the first round of judging.

We've also brought back our "Can They Do It?" pet talent competition, though with a few changes from last year. Our prizes remain at $100, $50, and $25, as they were, but we're restricting entry to four-legged creatures. And feces-throwing is no longer considered an acceptable talent, after Bobo, a chimpanzee belonging to Mary Mastroannio of Marketing, nearly blinded a child with a side-armed delivery.

New to our pet day will be the "Show Them Your Stuff" contest, to determine the dog or cat with the largest "scrotal package." Pets with implants are expressly excluded from the competition.

Days like this bring your families, and ours, the Stooples family, closer together. I look forward to a day of love, fun, and excitement. See you there.

Warning: For those of you who are a bit squeamish, please stop reading here:

And now, fathers, the moment you've all been waiting for: dogfights. Harry took the rap from the local DA on that bogus cruelty-to-animals charge for last year's death matches, which were broken up by the Newark Police. Unfortunately, at least one bleeding-heart, PETA-loving wife turned stoolpigeon, and we were caught, red-handed, in the parking lot.

This year, for privacy's sake, we're moving the dog pit into our basement. Entry will be by invitation only, one person at a time, no video or filming allowed. Dogs are to be brought around the back entrance. Keep them away from the beauty contest. You'll recall that last year, our second-place winner, a schnauzer named Mitzie, had her left leg ripped off by Colonel Klink, a four-year-old pit bull. The taste of blood appears to have done him well, though, as he made it through to the final before it was halted due to the police raid. In any case, we're offering on-site oddsmaking and cover for when your wife asks where you've gone. Four husbands have agreed to stand watch, saying things like, "Oh, Bob went out for a smoke" or "I think he had to tinkle," if anyone inquires.

Hope to see one and all there for the fun events and blood sport.

Regards,

Donny

SPECIAL $399⁹⁹

LEAVE Dallas
2:45pm
ARRIVE El Paso
1:58pm

Corporate Time Machine

Space Age device allows you to go back in time while you fly. Example: Leave Dallas 2:45 p.m., arrive El Paso 1:58 p.m. Or leave Gary 4:08 a.m., arrive Chicago 3:57 a.m.! Gives you up to 18 minutes to reevaluate your life, correct all your mistakes and get a second chance—just like in the movies. TimeZone differentiator not included. SKU **SECOND CHANCE**

Run with Scissors

No longer must you leave your scissors on your desk while you rush down the hall like they're giving free BJs in the bathroom. "Run with Scissors" races by your side wherever you go, clearing the hallway with amazing precision. Comfortable, polyrubber handles are made from the bald wigs of "before" patients from Miloxidal ads. Little screw in the middle that holds blades together made from real, uh, screw stuff. Lifetime warranty, unless you fall on them and kill yourself. SKU **BJS?**

$100
per 15 minute session

ONLY
$14⁹⁹

A WAY
TO STOP IT
$18,999⁹⁹

Rubic's Cubicle

Bored at work? Hours of fun await as you try to unravel the mystery of your Rubic's Cubicle. Where is your printer? Why is your coatrack upside down? Who is this angry clown sitting on your file cabinet? After you return your office to normal, your self-shuffling Rubic's Cubicle will rearrange all the furniture at lunchtime, and then CC all your e-mails to your ex-wife's lover. And it all begins again tomorrow!

Rumor Mill

Dull day? E-Z Crank Rumor Mill ® is just the thing for creating organizational havoc. Ordinary mill emits fortune cookie–style messages guaranteed to spread like wildfire: "The CEO has developed Alzheimer's and is now making good decisions," "Phone records from the cafeteria show 37 calls to the salmonella hotline," and "Our Canadian investors will make us play hockey at the next company picnic before they give us another round of financing." Specify Playful, Deceitful or Better Left Unsaid. SKU **SCUTTLEBUT**

Spread Havoc for ONLY
$44⁹⁹

  Visit us online @ **www.stooples.com**  Call 1-800-STOOPLE

Save $10

$389⁹⁵

Reg. $399.95

Hold Music Karaoke

Bored out of your mind as the Hold Music endlessly repeats "Wind Beneath My Wings"? Want to do something other than shoot Bette Midler out of a cannon? Don't shoot—join in! Hold Music Karaoke takes Bette and Whitney and other crooners out of the song, leaves just the music so you can take over. Digital phone display shows words and beat; lets you know when to hit the high notes and when to end with a loving whisper. Beeps 1.5 seconds before other party rejoins conversation, giving you time to compose yourself yet end with rousing finish. Tone deaf? Hold Music Karaoke earplugs available for office mates who just don't appreciate great music. Bette Midler not included. SKU **BFLAT**

Type Away CD

CD or audio cassette plays 60 minutes of computer tapping. Close the door, slip in player, enjoy a midday snooze. Convincing recording mixes short bursts of inspiration with hunt and peck. Deluxe recording adds disgusted crumpling of paper and stomping around office. Available in 90, 60 or 15 words per minute. SKU **ZZZZ**

Save $1

$4⁹⁹

Silent Partner Mime

You're not supposed to hear from silent partners, but that doesn't mean they can't be seen! Silent partner mime won't interfere in your management of operations, but will mimic business decisions while standing outside your front entrance. From "digging ourselves in a hole" to "cutting our losses" to "slicing the dividend," Silent Partner Mime provides hours of entertainment for your employees, suppliers, even investigative reporters. Our deluxe models will parody your best customers and the board of directors. Silent Partner Mime invested his capital, now he wants to have his fun! SKU **BLABBERMIME**

ONLY
$10,000⁰⁰

Corporate Religious Passage of the Day

Concerned that workers are guided more by faith than by company goals? Corporate Religious Passage of the Day can sway them to honor C-level executives as well as their maker. Examples: *"Thou Shalt Not Bear False Witness Unless the SEC Is Involved," "Oh, Glorious CEO, Please Take Another Jaw-Dropping $123 Million in Executive Compensation, Not Including a 23-Bedroom Castle in Lake Punta Gordo, Florida," "Thou Shalt Not Covet Thy Neighbor's Wife" or a "Jenna Jameson Screen Saver"* and many more. Corporate Scripture at its best! SKU **BLESSETHTHYCFO,TOO**

Only
$4⁹⁹
Per Quotation

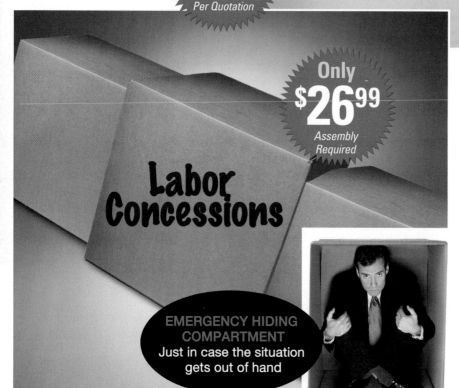

CORPORATE RELIGIOUS PASSAGE OF THE DAY

4:19
"Thou Shalt Not Bear False Witness Unless the SEC Is Involved,"

4:20
"Oh, Glorious CEO, Please Take Another Jaw-Dropping $123 Million in Executive Compensation, Not Including a 23-Bedroom Castle in Lake Punta Gordo, Florida,"

4:21
"Thou Shalt Not Covet Thy Neighbor's Wife or a Jenna Jameson Screen Saver."

Only
$26⁹⁹
Assembly Required

Labor Concessions

EMERGENCY HIDING COMPARTMENT
Just in case the situation gets out of hand

Labor Concession Stand

Union officials: No need to go to management's place to hand over benefits. Modular concession stand makes them line up for give backs. Cardboard construction folds quickly, transports to neutral locations for capitulation with dignity. Hidden drawer helps you hold on to dental plan to prevent rioting by union membership. SKU **SCAB**

M E M O

To: All Staff
From: The Chief of Card Holders
Re: New Drug Policy

All:

I'm proud to announce that after a sealed-bid auction, we've won a big contract to supply the Pentagon with all of its office needs. Though we won the auction because we were the low bidder, it's safe to say we'll make up in bulk what we might surrender on margins. I think the military was impressed that we were able to offer a price of $17.99 per paper clip and $199.95 per three-ring binder (without paper). I know our CFO, Julius de Krook, was.

This contract means we'll be acquiring a Washington, D.C., warehouse and opening a new satellite office there. Staff there will need to receive a security clearance, which will require a battery of tests and questioning from federal officers.

In a completely unrelated matter, please joint me in stamping out drugs at our fair company. I'm not talking about the occasional Tylenol for hangovers or the Midols you ladies pop for feminine discomfort. Oh, no. I'm talking about ganja, hash, goofballs, Bolivian marching powder, and the big "H." I'm sure none of that goes on at our fair company, especially not in the Number 6 Loading Dock area at around 11 p.m. each night, or the ladies' lavatory at coffee-break time.

Though I'm sure it's not necessary, we're also instituting random drug tests. They're not mandatory, but there's a high degree of probability that we'll be needing staff in our Hanoi office, where the tap water causes shooting diarrhea and the cockroaches will wrestle you for lunch, I'm told. Additionally, once he's released from drug rehab after inhaling a kilo of cocaine, we've arranged to borrow "Sniffles, the Wonder Beagle" from the U.S. Customs & Excise Department to sweep our offices for illicit drugs and related paraphernalia. Now people, I don't know about you, but wouldn't it suck to be bagged by a dog wearing a sweater?

Lastly, for those of you designated for security clearance, remember to tell anyone who might ask that we had no idea those Stooples shipping containers seized from Colombia last year were filled with unprocessed coca paste. Our lawyer says they were clearly tampered with. He also reminds staff that polygraphs are inadmissible in court and suggests repeating the answers to anticipated questions twenty-five times in your head, relaxing and taking deep breaths when you're hooked up to the machine. They're notoriously unreliable.

Regards and clean out those desk drawers with a Dustbuster,

Donny

Snivel Slacks

Keep your job no matter how incompetent you may be. Baggy, frayed corduroys will evoke pity in even the most steel-hearted employer. Quilted knee-pads allow you to grovel in comfort. Washed-out coloring delivers the coup de grâce, unmistakably showing your need for corporate compassion. SKU **SQUIRM**

ONLY
$69⁹⁹
Per Set

Time Sheet Pillow Cases

If you're thinking of the client at night, they deserve to be billed. New Time Sheet Pillow Cases let you record business activity even after you've gone to bed. Fidgeting under the covers about budget issues? Scratch one hour on pillow. Dreaming that "Naked Before the Client but Still Making the Presentation and They're Laughing at Me" dream? It's billable! Now when you say you're working 24/7, you really mean it! SKU **NIGHT SHIFT**

NEW
Low Price
$27⁹⁹

Handi-Shares

Soft, absorbent stock certificates from defunct silver mines, dot-coms and other firms that have gone down the toilet. Intricately patterned paper cleans spills and noses better than other two-ply certificates. Washable if bankruptcy proceedings reopen. Come 250 to a box, 400 a roll. SKU **WIPE**

$2⁹⁹
PER BOX

RÉSUMÉ

Ivana Bump
75 Trinity St., Apt. 5A
Route 43, Exit 16
Flatbush, NJ 09103
609-555-1234

OBJECTIVE: I try to be, though, like all possessors of a brilliant mind, it's hard to avoid creative and highly educated subjectivity and perceptiveness to creep into my deep and reasoned thoughts.

EDUCATION:
Montclair State University, B.A., Triple Major in Sociology, Art, and Sociology of Art, 1985.
Winnapaquot Jr. College, A.B., *magna cum laude*, in Automotive Repair, Geology, and Criminology, 1983.
DegreesUSA, Drawing by Mail Certificate in Water Colors and Cartoons, 1982.

WORK EXPERIENCE:
Stooples Inc., Newark, NJ—Purchasing Manager, 2002–present.
Work closely with and under top executives, including CEO, to fulfill this burgeoning office-supply company's needs. Developed "Buy What We Need" strategy that involves employees only buying what they need. Regularly rearranged closets to ensure we're not ordering things we don't need, but just can't find, because they're buried under other stuff. Extensive management-training experience and frequently got to use key to executive washrooms.

Stooples, Inc., Trenton, NJ—Stockroom Supervisor, 2000–2002
Hired as stockroom assistant, enacted bold and aggressive action plans, including adding third shelf to two-shelf warehouse shelving units. Rose quickly to supervisor post after torrid affair with previous stockroom supervisor, accusing him of sexual harassment, and taking his job when he resigned in disgrace and committed suicide.

Bennie's Auto Parts, Flatbush, NJ—Executive Secretary to CEO, 1996–1999
Operated complex telecommunications switchboard equipment, learned to write really fast with phone cradled on my shoulder and type with four fingers, not just two. Unparalleled efficiency at taking doughnut and sandwich orders, able to hear and transmit phone messages over whine of grease gun. Proficiency at replacing tires, oil, wiper blades, and other minor auto repairs.

Rahway State Prison for Women, Rahway, NJ—Prison Guard, 1994–1996
Successfully processed over 3,200 prisoners, including 24 "Big Bad Mamas" and 16 "Dykes on Bikes." Prevented approximately 1,300 pounds of illegal or contraband material from entering prison, including pornography, alcohol, birth control, men, "men substitutes," small farm animals, and various weapons and foodstuffs. Twice voted "Glove of the Year," for prowess at conducting cavity searches.

SPECIAL SKILLS: Can touch the tip of my tongue to the tip of my nose. Know how to burp the alphabet, not only forward, but backward as well. Can put legs behind my head after several minutes of warm-up stretching. Uncanny ability to estimate numbers accurately, from forks in a drawer to beans in a jar. Can apply nail polish with applicator held between my teeth.

LANGUAGES: Beginning Español, Some Langue de l'Amour, and fluent Ebonics.

HOBBIES: Motorcycle racing, target shooting, amateur piercing, contemplating the Universe.

STOoPLES
Office Tools for Hopeless Fools

Donny Steintrumper
Chairman & CEO
Stooples Inc.
232 S. Pitt Rd.
Newark, NJ 07310-5651

Terry Hudson
General Manager
West Virginia Slags Basketball Team
Mt. St. Bernard's Girls' Catholic High School Gym
Bud, West Virginia 24716

March 22, 2004

Dear Ter:

At the end of a rather tumultuous season, I have to say you've quite astonished me. I didn't think any sports team anywhere could play worse or be valued any lower than the West Virginia Slags when I bought them. But with you calling the shots and handling the draft and other player transactions, you've proved me wrong.

While it's not your fault that the Continental Basketball Association folded, leaving us without an arena, opponents, or any means to meet payroll, who else can I blame for the failure to negotiate concessions rights with the nuns at Mt. St. Bernard's Catholic High School? Dammit, man, we may not be able to charge for luxury boxes, but every homemade brownie and cup of lukewarm lemonade counts. And we won't even talk about how you let the good sisters' claptrap about "un-Christian behavior" deter you from installing pay toilets and introducing valet parking on the school campus.

You should have also known that the Yao Ming you drafted wasn't the 7'6" basketball player for the Houston Rockets, but a 4'11" basket weaver from Hunan province, who only fits into a Peewee League uniform, doesn't speak a word of English, and grosses out the other team by blowing his nose on the floor, hocking up green goobers from his lungs, and walking around with acupuncture needles stuck in his head. Congratulations for locking him in with a seven-year, $22 million contract.

I could overlook all of that, provided you had at least met me halfway in my quest to secure public funds for a new arena in beautiful downtown Bud and a spot in the WNBA. Though I handpicked opponents for you—and despite my best efforts to help—the team continued to lose, diminishing our chances for either of those things to happen.

We were lucky enough to squeak by with a tie against that wheelchair basketball team after the lights suddenly went out in the third quarter and all fuses in the fuse box mysteriously disappeared. Unforgivable was that loss in the final game of the season against the Calcutta Lepers. For crying out loud, they were—literally—half the team that we were.

Ter, I'm very sorry, but I'm a results man, and you've simply not produced them. I hope you'll remain a Slags fan, but one who buys a ticket from the ninth-grader manning the door. So, see you around and take your coaching staff and players with you. You're fired—and your entire coaching staff and players, too.

Yours,

Donny

Donny Steintrumper
Chairman & CEO
Stooples Inc.
232 S. Pitt Rd.
Newark, NJ 07310-5651

Mr. Cazimir Cwzrskskszski
Sports Agent
Pije Kuba Polka Agency
21 Marshal Pilsudski Drive
Warsaw, Poland

Dear Mr. Cwzrskskszski:

It was a pleasure speaking with you on the phone the other day. I had absolutely no idea what the hell you were talking about and in what language you were saying it, but it was a pleasure nonetheless.

I understand through some acquaintances of mine that you represent a large stable of talented Polish athletes, if that's not a contradiction in terms. I have a business proposition for you. I want them. All of them. Right away. Signed to five-year contracts.

Let me back up for a second. I'm a billionaire businessman. I'm chairman and CEO of that famous American office-supply company Stooples, which has an office and factory in your lovely country. Perhaps you've heard of us? Anyway, I digress. I also own the West Virginia Slags, an up-and-coming professional basketball team that finds itself with about twelve openings for players.

That's where you and your clients come in. I need about twelve of them, as tall as you can get. If they already know how to play baskeball, that's a plus. But I'd be willing to take soccer, badminton, tennis, and any other players you represent, provided they look good in a uniform and don't understand the concept of "free agency."

I'm offering equally generous terms to all of them—a concept that, as former Communists, I'm sure they'll appreciate. Each will get a green card that allows them to work in the United States. They'll be paid $5.25 an hour, not just on the nights when they play games, but also for practices. We'll supply them with Dunkin' Donuts vouchers for breakfast, a peanut butter or ham sandwich for lunch, and a hot dinner at Denny's or an equivalent restaurant each day. We'll provide double trailers parked at the foothills of the Ozark Mountains, two players per trailer. Since we play in a girls' Catholic school, your clients can rest assured there are lots of nuns for those who need spiritual guidance and lots of young and impressionable Catholic girls in plaid skirts and knee socks for those who don't. All travel will be done on first-class buses supplied by the Peter Pan company. We'll supply uniforms and gymsuits. I'm also offering bonuses of $5 per player for every win.

Mr. Cwzrskskszski, I hope you and your clients will take me up on this attractive offer and join my basketball team for its upcoming season. We should soon have a new coach on board, and I know he's eager to start training camp with a player or two. Please let me know, and you might consider buying a vowel.

Sincerely,

Donny Steintrumper

Donny Steintrumper
Chairman & CEO
Stooples Inc.
232 S. Pitt Rd.
Newark, NJ 07310-5651

Mr. Cazimir Cwzrskskszski
Sports Agent
Pije Kuba Polka Agency
21 Marshal Pilsudski Drive
Warsaw, Poland

Dear Caz:

If we're to be on a first-name basis, call me Donny, or "the Basketball Stud."

Tell your clients if they can get in on a family-day pass, no problem. Otherwise, the best I can do is Universal Studios, which offers discounts to groups of ten and more.

Regards,

Donny

P.S. Vowels are letters like a,e,i,o,u and sometimes y, which make words and names actually pronounceable.

Mr. Cazimir Cwzrskskszski
Sports Agent
Pije Kuba Polka Agency
21 Marshal Pilsudski Drive
Warsaw, Poland

Donny Szsctzceintrzszsumpzsczer
Chairman & CEO
Stooples Inc.
232 S. Pitt Rd.
Newark, NJ 07310-5651

Dear Mr. Szsctzceintrzszsumpzsczer:

Players ask if they can have trip to Disney World.

Sincerely,

Caz

P.S. What is "vowel"?

Mr. Cazimir Cwzrskskszski
Sports Agent
Pije Kuba Polka Agency
21 Marshal Pilsudski Drive
Warsaw, Poland

Donny Trzszsumpzsczcteiner
Chairman & CEO
Stooples Inc.
232 S. Pitt Rd.
Newark, NJ 07310-5651

Dear Basczketczsball Stud:

You have deal. My boys ready to dunk slam for you.

Cheers,

Caz

STOOPLES
Office Tools for Hopeless Fools

Donny Steintrumper
Chairman & CEO
Stooples Inc.
232 S. Pitt Rd.
Newark, NJ 07310-5651

Bobby Knight
Varsity Basketball Coach
Texas Tech University

Dear Mr. Knight:

I've long been an admirer of your coaching skills and ability to sling folding chairs across the width of the basketball court on blown calls by the referee. You look great in a sweater, with its bright-red shade exactly matching your face when you're pissed off. I'd like to offer you a job.

I'm the owner of the West Virginia Slags, an up-and-coming professional team that has only Polish players and works for minimum wage. I need somebody who can teach them a few good swear words and a few basketball moves before our regular season starts. Your reputation precedes you, and I'd be honored if you'd take over my team as coach and general manager.

You'd have absolute control over player and personnel decisions, meaning you can bring in as many short, slow white guys as you want, though we expect our Polish contingent will have more than a few you might like.

In any case, I can assure you of a substantial raise and far more control of a basketball program than you've ever had to date. Also, you can smack our players around because we'll threaten to pull their green cards if they complain to the authorities. I'll also never get mad at you for recruiting violations or losing your temper. On the contrary, like you, I'll do anything to win, and I've thrown a few chairs in my lifetime, let me tell you.

I hope that before you make up your mind that you'll come and visit me on my yacht. I'll wine and dine you and ply you with expensive hookers all night until you say yes.

I look forward to hearing from you.

Regards,

Donny Steintrumper

Christmas Cookies Incinerator

You've gained 40 pounds over the holidays and people are still bringing their damn Christmas cookies to work. Show them you've had enough with Desktop Christmas Cookie Incinerator. Accepts tins, jars and platefuls of cookies in environmentally efficient, thermal-powered combustion chamber. Keeps hazardous cookies out of landfills, eliminates need for ocean dumping. Odorless, smokeless and tasteless. Not endorsed by Santa or any of his helpers. SKU **NUFF ALREADY**

Geese a-Layin' Screen Saver

What better way to spend your Internet holiday season than to watch eggs pop out of geese! Our holiday screen saver is the perfect gift for country cousins who enjoy watching animals procreate and always wondered what happens next. Specify slo-mo, quick delivery or eggs a-bouncin'. SKU **PLOP!**

$11⁹⁹

HOLIDAY GIFT IDEAS
from Stooples

Santa 'Plause

Only $26.99

When Santa makes a perfect three-point pirouette down the chimney, is he sad that no one sees it? Our Santa 'Plause motion detector responds immediately to Santa touchdown, activates wild applause and cheering recorded from Broadway shows, Super Bowl touchdowns and when Jane McCallister took off her top at the office Christmas party. Soft enough not to wake the little ones, but high-pitched enough to get on reindeer nerves. No more Sulky Santa!

SKU **JANE DID WHAT?**

First Day of Christmas Insurance

On the first day of Christmas—what if the goddamned partridge dies? What will you tell the three French hens, let alone the eleven lords a-leapin'? Protect holiday season continuity with First Day of Christmas Insurance from LibertyMusical. Comprehensive policy guarantees animal replacement within hours with similar-looking pigeon, moose or Rwandan refugee. Also available: Replacement Maids a-Milkin' (specify callous or noncallous). SKU **ELEVEN INSURANCE MEN INSURANCING**

ONLY $999.99

Protect holiday season continuity with First Day of Christmas Insurance from Liberty Musical.

Christmas-Dinner Fork Net

Save $2

$8.95
Reg. $10.95

People make such pigs of themselves at holiday dinners. Small mesh fork net fits easily under utensil so food stays out of your lap. No more Brussels sprouts bouncing off your knee onto the floor where Aunt Sarah was walking, culminating in her hip replacement. No sir, just periodically empty your fork net back onto your plate and get ready for more clumsy eating! Also available: Spoon Pool. SKU **FORK YOU**

 STOOPLES
Office Tools for Hopeless Fools

 Visit us online @ **www.stooples.com**

 Call **1-800-STOOPLE**

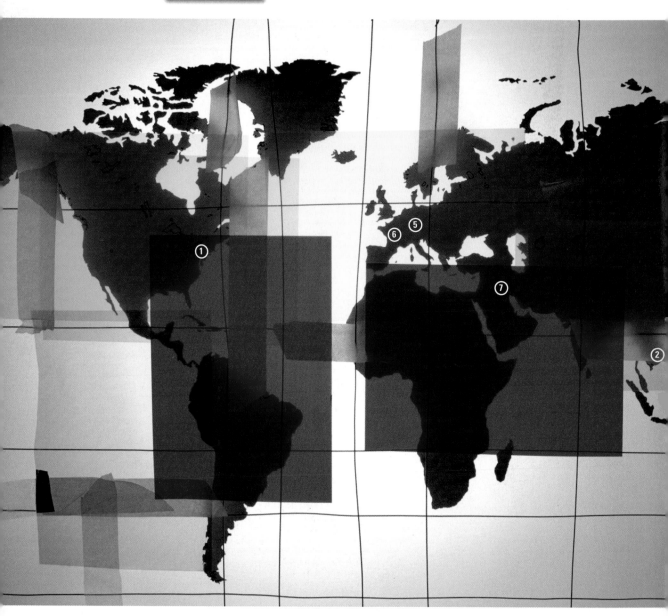

Stooples is proud to offer top-quality office products from 38 showrooms across the United States and via mail order. We also operate overseas in 7 countries, though we don't really consider Canada a country. In addition to legal products, we sell gray-market items and price-dump illegally in 23 countries, without having been caught or fined even once. We want your business and offer fantastic deals, until you read the fine print. Please write or visit us at the following locations.

  Visit us online @ **www.stooples.com**  **Call 1-800-STOOPLE**